Goldfish WITHDRAWN

2nd Edition

GET MORE!
Visit www.wiley.com/
go/goldfish

Gregory Skomal, PhD

Wiley Publishing, Inc.

Howell Book House

Published by Wiley Publishing, Inc., Hoboken, New Jersey

Library of Congress Cataloging-in-Publication Data:
Skomal, Gregory.
  Goldfish / Gregory Skomal. -- 2nd ed.
    p. cm. -- (Your happy healthy pet)
  Rev. ed. of: Goldfish / [Carlo De Vito with Gregory Skomal]. c1996.
  ISBN-13: 978-0-470-16512-6 (cloth)
  1. Goldfish. I. DeVito, Carlo. Goldfish. II. Title.
  SF458.G6D4 2007
  639.3'7484--dc22
                          2007020115
Printed in the United States of America

10 9 8 7 6 5 4 3 2 1

Book design by Melissa Auciello-Brogan
Cover design by Michael J. Freeland
Book production by Wiley Publishing, Inc. Composition Services
Wiley Bicentennial Logo: Richard J. Pacifico

About the Author

Gregory Skomal, PhD, is an accomplished marine biologist, underwater explorer, photographer, aquarist, and author. He has been a fisheries biologist with the Massachusetts Division of Marine Fisheries since 1987 and currently heads up the Massachusetts Shark Research Program. He has written numerous scientific research papers and has appeared in a number of film and television shark documentaries, including programs for National Geographic and Discovery Channel.

Although his research passion for the last 24 years has been sharks, he is also an avid aquarist and has written numerous books on aquarium keeping. His home and laboratory are on the island of Martha's Vineyard off the coast of Massachusetts.

About Howell Book House

Since 1961, Howell Book House has been America's premier publisher of pet books. We're dedicated to companion animals and the people who love them, and our books reflect that commitment. Our stable of authors—training experts, veterinarians, breeders, and other authorities—is second to none. And we've won more Maxwell Awards from the Dog Writers Association of America than any other publisher.

As we head toward the half-century mark, we're more committed than ever to providing new and innovative books, along with the classics our readers have grown to love. From bringing home a new puppy to competing in advanced equestrian events, Howell has the titles that keep animal lovers coming back again and again.

Contents

Shopping List

You'll need to do a bit of stocking up before you bring your goldfish home. Below is a basic list of must-have supplies. For more detailed information on the selection of each item below, consult chapters 4 and 5. For specific guidance on what food you'll need, review chapter 7.

☐ Tank

☐ Tank stand

☐ Hood

☐ Filter

☐ Water-quality test kit

☐ Air pump

☐ Airstones

☐ Air hose

☐ Thermometer

☐ Heater

☐ Gravel

☐ Plants

☐ Algal cleaner

☐ Aquarium vacuum

☐ Fish net

☐ 5-gallon bucket

☐ Siphon hose

☐ Fish food

There are likely to be a few other items that, depending upon your aquarium setup, you may wish to pick up before bringing your goldfish home. Use the blank spaces at the end of this list to note any additional items you'll be shopping for.

☐ _____

☐ _____

☐ _____

☐ _____

☐ _____

☐ _____

☐ _____

☐ _____

☐ _____

☐ _____

Pet Sitter's Guide

We can be reached at (___)_____-_____ Cell phone (___)_____-_____

We will return on _____ (date) at _____ (approximate time)

Other individual to contact in case of emergency _____

Goldfish species: _____

Care Instructions

In the following blank lines, let the sitter know what to feed, how much, and when; what tasks need to be performed daily; and what weekly tasks they'll be responsible for.

Morning _____

_____

_____

_____

_____

_____

Evening _____

_____

_____

_____

_____

_____

Other tasks and special instructions _____

_____

_____

_____

_____

_____

_____

Part I
All About Goldfish

The Goldfish

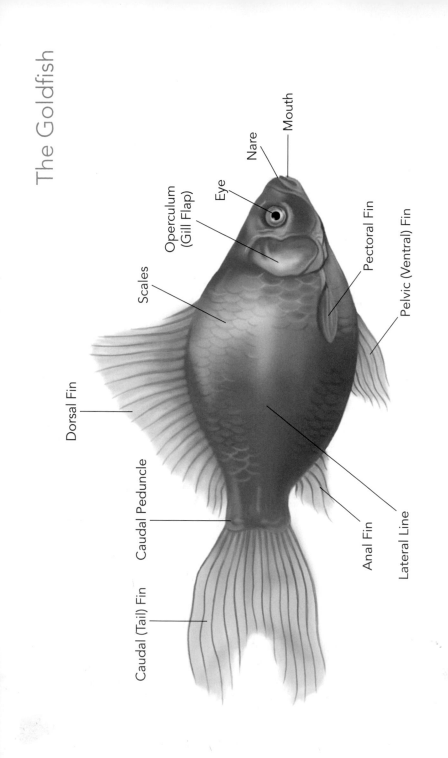

Mouth

Nare

Eye

Operculum
(Gill Flap)

Scales

Pectoral Fin

Pelvic (Ventral) Fin

Dorsal Fin

Caudal Peduncle

Anal Fin

Lateral Line

Caudal (Tail) Fin

Chapter 1

What Is a Goldfish?

The popular image of a goldfish in a bowl has been depicted the world over—from Chinese Ming Dynasty pottery to popular comic strips such as *Garfield*. Goldfish are the most popular domesticated aquatic life in the world, and there are more than 125 varieties—more varieties than any other fish species.

All of these varieties are thought to have been bred from a single species, the Crucian carp. These fish are long, flat-sided, and generally look like drab gray goldfish. The goldfish of today tend to be more colorful than their ancestors.

Regardless of variety, the goldfish is one of the most popular pets in the world. Goldfish don't need to be housebroken, they won't beg at the table, and they don't shed. They're flexible about the size of their aquarium, which can depend on the size of the room, and they're easy to keep.

Another great thing about goldfish is that they are a fairly hardy species and are quite adaptable. They are excellent candidates for outdoor ponds or pools in almost any climate. Given the wide range of colors, body shapes, and general disposition, there is a goldfish out there for everyone.

The History of Goldfish

For centuries, the Crucian carp and its various progeny were found only in Asia and were particularly prized in China and, some time later, in Japan. The Chinese word for goldfish is *jin yü*. Goldfish were first mentioned in China during the first Jin Dynasty (265–420). Some 500 years later, during the Song

Classifying Goldfish

Goldfish, scientifically known as *Carassius auratus*, can still be found in streams and ponds throughout Asia. In the wild, their colors are somewhat muddy and drab. The goldfish belongs to the largest family of fishes in the world, the Cyprinidae, which contains more than 2,000 species, including such common aquarium fishes as Barbs and Danios. The closest relatives of the goldfish are the Crucian carp (*Carassius carassius*) and the Koi (*Cyprinus carpio*).

The best way to distinguish between a carp and a goldfish is to look at the dorsal fin, which is usually straight up or concave (curved in) on the goldfish and convex (curved out) on the carp.

There are also some differences between Koi and goldfish that are easy to spot. Koi have very similar coloration, except that they have larger patches of color on the body. Also, while the Common Goldfish, which is the largest of all goldfish, rarely grows longer than 12 to 14 inches, Koi routinely grow to 18 inches and have been seen as long as almost 4 feet. But the easiest way to distinguish between goldfish and Koi is simple: Koi have small, nubbly whiskers (called barbels) on the sides of their mouth and underneath their chin. These barbels do not grow very long, but they are noticeable all the same.

How Scientists Classify Goldfish

Class:	Actinopterygii
Order:	Cypriniformes
Family:	Cyprinidae
Genus:	*Carassius*
Species:	*Auratus*

Dynasty (960–1279), it was not uncommon to have ornamental domesticated fish. These were usually kept in ponds or pools in courtyards and gardens.

The species was so popular in China, particularly in Beijing, that during the second Jin Dynasty (1115–1234) a goldfish pool was established in the capital city for commercial breeding. Goldfish reached such a height of popularity during the Ming Dynasty (1368–1644) that they were no longer a luxury for the privileged. Many courtyard gardens had ponds with ornamental goldfish, and they were even brought inside in clay pots. It was very common to keep successful breeding techniques a secret.

The big fish in this pond is a Koi and the smaller ones are goldfish.

Goldfish reached Japan in 1616, and the Japanese also became quite enamored of these beautiful fish. They quickly mastered the art of breeding them, and Koriyama, on the Japanese island of Honshu, has been one of the most famous goldfish breeding centers for more than 500 years. Japan is now the largest exporter of goldfish worldwide.

The Chinese and Japanese produced the Fantail, the Veiltail, the Globe-Eyed, and the varieties with transparent scales. Some of these varieties can be traced as far back as the late sixteenth and early seventeenth centuries.

In 1691, goldfish appeared in mainland Europe. From there they arrived in England in 1780. During the eighteenth century, as trade with the British, French, Dutch, and Portuguese flourished, goldfish became fashionable gifts and pets throughout Western Europe. By

> **Born in the USA**
>
> Despite there being more than 125 varieties of goldfish, the United States has only contributed one variety to this ever-popular species— the Comet. It was bred here by Hugo Murkett and the U.S. Fisheries Department around 1881. While it is the only variety bred on American shores at the time of this writing, with the numerous breeding centers around the nation, America's contribution could grow at any time.

Ornamental goldfish have been kept and bred in China for more than 1,000 years.

1850, goldfish arrived in the New World, and they were a big attraction in New York in 1865.

Keeping tropical fish became truly popular in the West after the opening of the first public aquarium at the London Zoo in 1853. The first goldfish show took place in Osaka, Japan, in 1862. The first goldfish show in the West took place in 1926 and was organized by the British Aquarists Association in London.

The Basic Goldfish Body

Although they all belong to the same species, there are more than 125 varieties of goldfish, and some look as different as cats and dogs. The Comet is the classic example of a common goldfish. The Comet's body is streamlined and tapers toward the head and the tail. The narrow section where the body meets the tail is the caudal peduncle. Regardless of variety, the caudal peduncle is almost always narrow on a goldfish, no matter how large the body. Some Fantail varieties, though, such as the Redcap and the Marigold Chinese Lionhead, have exceptionally large heads, while Moors and Veiltails, which are quite round, vary in their head shapes and sizes.

However, there are some features that are common to all goldfish—and are found in all fish. For example, although goldfish look very different from other tropical fishes, they have circulatory, respiratory, digestive, and nervous systems common to most members of this vertebrate group.

Fins

The fins are critically important appendages that enable every fish to propel itself, stabilize, maneuver, and stop. There are typically two types of fins, paired (one fin on either side of the body) and unpaired, and they are found at five places on the fish's body. To have a better idea of where these fins are located on a typical goldfish, look at the drawing on page 10.

The pectoral fins are the paired fins closest to the head. The fish uses these fins to stabilize itself, turn, maneuver, hover, and swim backwards. These fins are generally found just behind or below the gills on each side of the fish, under the midline of the body. On goldfish, the pectoral fins are different shapes on different varieties. They can be short and small, as on a Lionhead, or long and flowing, as on a Veiltail.

The pelvic fins are also paired; different fish have them in very different places. In some fish, these fins are under the fish toward the rear. In others, like the goldfish, the pelvic fins are closer to the head under the pectorals. The pelvic

Every fish has fins to propel itself, stabilize, maneuver, and stop. This is a Fantail.

fins act as brakes and also aid in stabilizing and turning the fish. In some varieties of goldfish, the pelvic fins may be elongated, as on a Veiltail Ryunkin.

The dorsal fin is an unpaired fin rising directly from the top of the middle of the fish's back. It is made of rigid spines and soft rays webbed with a membrane. The dorsal fin helps stabilize the fish right-side up and keeps it moving straight. When a goldfish is healthy, this fin stands straight up. Some varieties of goldfish, such as the Celestial, have no dorsal fin, and consequently have more difficulty swimming.

The anal fin protrudes from the bottom of the body, just in front of the tail. This unpaired fin works in concert with the dorsal fin to stabilize the fish. On some varieties of goldfish, the anal fin aids in propulsion and turning in small spaces. In some of the fancy varieties, the anal fin splits into a set of paired fins that are actually joined together where they meet the body. In the fancier varieties, the anal fin is so exaggerated that it is not very useful, and consequently these fish are bad swimmers.

The caudal, or tail, fin is an unpaired fin largely responsible for propelling the fish forward. It can also act as a brake, but is much more helpful in turning. There are three types of caudal fins: the single tail fin, the veiltail, and the fantail. The single tail fin is obvious and can be found on the common goldfish. The fantail is the most common of the fancy varieties and is a pair of forked tails joined at the caudal peduncle. The veiltail is a beautiful, large tail that has no indentations or forks and ends in a straight line; it is generally very long and elegant.

Scales

The body of a goldfish is covered with overlapping scales that are made of a hard, bony substance. They protect the fish's skin, reducing the chance of injuries or infection. The scales of a fish are translucent, like glass, and lack color; the color of the goldfish comes from pigment cells in the deeper dermal layer of skin. The forward end of each scale is attached to the dermis—the skin. The scales overlap like shingles on a house, providing a solid wall of protection.

The scales are covered by epidermal tissue that has numerous glands that secrete mucus and produce the slimy texture we normally attribute to fish. The mucous coating not only protects the fish against injury and infection, but also helps reduce friction between the body and the water, enabling the fish to swim more easily.

Much like tree rings, for each season of growth in a goldfish (a growth season is approximately one year, provided there is a six- to eight-week drop in temperature), the goldfish develops a ring on its scales. These rings are called circuli. The number of rings on the scale determines the age of the fish.

Scale Types

Goldfish can be characterized based on four scale types:

- **Metallic.** Fish with metallic scales have a shiny, scaly exterior, such as is seen in the Comet. These scales contain a crystalline substance called guanine, which is responsible for the sheen; the more guanine, the shinier the scale.
- **Matte.** Matte scales lack guanine almost entirely and have no reflective surfaces anywhere on the fish's body. Instead, they have a flat or skinlike look to them. Truly matte-type goldfish are typically not available commercially because they lack intensive coloration and are not as hardy as other fish. Matte fish are sometimes referred to as scaleless. This is incorrect—there is no such thing as a scaleless goldfish.
- **Nacreous.** When both metallic and matte scales are found on a goldfish, it is known as nacreous. Some individual scales, or whole sections of the body, might have a metallic-type finish, while others might have a matte-type finish.
- **Calico.** This category classifies any goldfish with three or more colors appearing anywhere on the body. Technically, this is not a scale type because scales do not have color, but it is often used to refer to goldfish with multiple colors. Many experts believe calico goldfish are really part of the nacreous group.

This Ryunkin goldfish has nacreous scales and a round body type.

> ## Sleep and Color
>
> If there is quiet time in your home, usually at night, you may find your fish resting at the bottom of the tank among some rocks or plants. Occasionally, the pectoral or tail fins will move to keep the fish balanced. Since they have no eyelids, many people think the fish are always awake. Wrong! They're asleep.
>
> Goldfish tend to lose some color and luster when they're sleeping. But don't worry—it comes right back when they wake up. In fact, to grow to their potential and have their best color, goldfish should have room to exercise and time to sleep. Goldfish need their rest, just like you, so turn the aquarium and room lights off during the evening hours and let your fish sleep. If you don't turn the light off, the fish will sleep for shorter periods of time or largely go without, which could result in shorter lifespan, less color, and less active fish.

Color

The coloration of a goldfish, or any fish for that matter, depends on a wide variety of factors. Of course, genetics plays a part. Water composition, temperature, and diet also greatly affect a fish's chromatophores (pigment cells). There are two types of chromatophores, melanophores and xanthophores. Orange goldfish have an abundance of xanthophores and an absence of melanophores, while the blue or black varieties, such as the Black Moor, have an abundance of melanophores and lack xanthophores.

How Do Goldfish Swim?

The back-and-forth movement of the caudal fin provides the goldfish with forward motion. The fish literally pulls its tail from one side of its body to the other. By going back and forth, the tail pushes the water behind it, thus creating thrust and pushing the fish forward. By bending the tail in subtle ways, the fish can also steer.

The fish stops by reversing the tail motion, quickly. All other fins immediately become rigid. Sometimes the pectoral fins are instrumental in backing up or when a sudden stop is needed, much like a thruster rocket on a spaceship.

The tail fin propels the fish forward, and the swim bladder enables the fish to rise or sink in the water.

Swim Bladder

The swim bladder is a gas-filled sac that helps a fish rise or fall in its watery environment. Goldfish actually have two swim bladders, one directly in front of the other. These compartments contain oxygen, carbon dioxide, and nitrogen.

By inflating and deflating its swim bladder, the goldfish controls its buoyancy. This also helps the fish stabilize and hover comfortably. Some of the more elaborate varieties of goldfish are top-heavy, and as a result will always swim at an angle. For example, the Lionhead has a smaller forward sac, causing its head to thrust slightly downward.

How Do Goldfish Breathe?

Goldfish, like all fish, need oxygen to live. Since they live in the water, they do not breathe air as we do. Instead of lungs, they have gills. Most fish have four gills on each side of the head protected by a single gill flap, or operculum. When a fish breathes, water is taken into the mouth and passed over the gills and out the operculum. As water passes over the membranes and filaments of the gills, oxygen is taken into the blood and carbon dioxide is excreted. Large amounts of ammonia are also excreted by the gills. To accomplish this, the gills have a very high number of blood vessels that deliver the oxygen to the rest of the fish via the circulatory system.

When there is not enough oxygen in the water, fish rise to just below the surface, where oxygen concentrations are greatest. These fish are actually trying to avoid suffocation. This occurs most often in the well-known goldfish bowl. We will talk about the dangers and problems of the goldfish bowl in chapter 4.

A Goldfish's Senses

Goldfish have five senses that they use to eat, avoid predators, communicate, and reproduce. Their senses are specially adapted to their underwater life.

Smell

A goldfish, like all fishes, has nostrils called nares. But, unlike us, goldfish cannot breathe through their nose. Their nares, located above the mouth and in front of or below the eyes, allow water to pass into and out of the olfactory organs. Water flows through the nares and into the olfactory pits, where odors are perceived and communicated to the brain via a large nerve. For goldfish, the sense of smell is particularly important in detecting prey and mates.

Touch

Fish have a special sensory organ called the lateral line system that enables them to detect movement in the water. The lateral line is easily visible along the side of the goldfish. It is a series of pits and grooves containing sensory cells that detect water displacement. This system helps the goldfish detect other fish and avoid obstacles.

Hearing

Water is a much more efficient conductor of sound than air. Therefore, sound carries much farther and faster in water than in air. The goldfish, like most fish, does not have external ears, but rather an inner ear structure consisting of the sacculus and the lagena, which house the sensory components of hearing, the otoliths. Sound vibrations pass through the water, through the fish, and reverberate in the otoliths of the inner ear. This gives a goldfish its sense of hearing and, like our own inner ear, its sense of balance. We know for sure that fish make sounds during eating, fighting, and mating, so hearing is essential for goldfish survival.

A fish's eyes are much like our own, except they lack eyelids. Most fish are nearsighted.

Sight

The eyes of most fish are similar to our own, except that they lack eyelids and their irises open and close much more slowly. Rapid changes in light intensity therefore tend to shock a fish—a fact you should keep in mind. Gradual changes in light enable the fish to accommodate and avoid temporary blindness.

The location of the spherical lenses of fish eyes renders most fish nearsighted. This is not a great handicap, since visibility in ponds and lakes is not always very good. Goldfish are able to detect color and, since their eyes are on either side of their heads, they have monocular vision as opposed to binocular vision like us.

The eyes are efficient at spotting food and dangers, including other fish. Highly developed goldfish varieties, which have bubble eyes or telescope eyes, are thought to see only upward. The Bubble Eye variety, which has large fluid sacs underneath its eyes, is thought to suffer vision loss as well. Despite this, these varieties of goldfish, when maintained with ordinary care, suffer no great problems when housed with other goldfish of the same type.

Taste

Most of a goldfish's tastebuds are located on the lips and all over the mouth. There are even taste buds on the outsides of the lips. Goldfish have no tongue. Taste in fish is especially helpful in identifying both food and noxious substances.

Chapter 2

(Almost) Endless Variety

There are no official divisions among the varieties of goldfish, but there are ways that goldfish enthusiasts group them. The groupings help aquarists understand something about these fish, their needs, and what other fish they might peacefully coexist with. For example, the Comet, the Common Goldfish, and the Shubunkin (both Bristol and London types) are all in the same group. These are strong, hardy swimmers, competitive fish, and should definitely not be kept with a Lionhead or Veiltail—slower swimmers who will not be able to compete for food. Consult your local aquarium store dealer before pairing fish that are not in the same group.

There are two basic goldfish body types. The first is the flat body type, including the Common Goldfish, the Comet, and the Shubunkin. The second is the round or egg-shaped body type, such as the Oranda and the Veiltail.

The following is a small sample of the many different types of goldfish. Many of these are commercially available, but some are quite rare.

Flat Body Type

These goldfish are among the hardiest of all the varieties. They are the fastest swimmers and the most streamlined. As a result, they are very competitive and successful when hunting for food. These goldfish tend to be extremely easy to care for, and therefore are excellent choices for beginners. These varieties are also generally better for ponds because they are robust and they tend to grow the largest.

Common Goldfish can grow to more than a foot long.

Common Goldfish

The Common Goldfish is the hardiest of all goldfish. Its life expectancy is somewhere between five and ten years, if it is properly maintained. These goldfish are ideal for outdoor ponds since they are able to withstand great temperature changes, from as low as 40°F to as high as 80°F.

Long, sleek, and flat-bodied, the Common Goldfish is the closest cousin to the carp. When young, it tends to be a bluish color. As the fish ages, it changes to a metallic orange.

The body of the Common Goldfish is tapered at the head and caudal peduncle, but is deeper and wider than that of the Comet. This goldfish has an erect dorsal fin, a single forked tail, and well-proportioned pectoral and ventral fins. As is typical of this group, these goldfish are fast swimmers and very competitive. They can grow as large as 12 to 14 inches in a pond and 6 to 9 inches in a large aquarium, depending on the size of the tank.

The Comet

The Comet is the only goldfish variety to have originated in the United States. Comets live in the reflecting pond on the Mall in Washington, D.C.

The Comet looks very much like a Common Goldfish, except that it is generally longer and sleeker and has more exaggerated fins. The fins are proportionally twice as long as those of a Common Goldfish, but the fin types are the same.

The Comet is the only American variety. This is an albino.

The tail fin is especially large and beautiful, sometimes as large as or larger than the body.

Comets come in silver (also known as white) and yellow, as well as in combinations of these colors. While they are usually metallic, nacreous Comets are not at all uncommon.

Like the Common Goldfish, the Comet is a fast swimmer, very hardy, and able to withstand great changes in temperature (40°F to 80°F). Comets are also excellent pond or aquarium fish, but they are somewhat smaller than Common Goldfish, growing to about 7 to 10 inches in length.

Shubunkin

Originally thought to be bred in Japan around the turn of the century, these fish became very popular in Britain. The name Shubunkin is Japanese, and means "deep red with different colors." In some circles, this fish is also known as the Harlequin.

Basically, the Shubunkin is a Common Goldfish that is calico or nacreous. They are long, sleek, and flat-sided. Their most attractive feature is the variety of hues. The colors are mostly deep reds, yellows, whites, and dark blues, violets, or blacks. Usually, the more dark colors a Shubunkin has, the more valuable it is in the marketplace.

This is a Bristol Shubunkin, showing off the wide variety of colors.

There are two types of Shubunkins: the London and the Bristol. The Bristol's tail fin is much larger than that of the London. The Bristol has a forked, wide tail that is not very long, while the more popular London variety has a smaller, more squared-off tail.

Shubunkins grow to a maximum size of about 6 inches, and are excellent swimmers. With proper care, the Shubunkin is one of the most long-lived of all domestic fish, living sometimes between ten and twenty years. They are ideal for outdoor pools and ponds and are hardy enough to withstand the broad temperature changes that occur throughout the year.

Wakin

The Wakin is the common goldfish of Japan, although this variety was first developed in China. Bluish in color when very young, it will grow to a deep vermillion red. Some strains of this variety have white patches. In all respects, the Wakin is very much like the Common Goldfish, except that it has a double caudal fin. Despite the double tail, the Wakin swims fast enough to be kept with other single-tailed, flat-bodied fish.

Jikin

The Jikin is also known as the Butterfly Tail Goldfish or the Peacock-Tailed Goldfish. It is very similar to the Wakin in all respects and is thought to be bred from the Wakin. The major difference is the tail, which, when fully opened, forms a large X and looks very much like a butterfly. These are hardy, good starter fish, but are not as easy to find as Common Goldfish or Comets.

Tancho Singletail

There is little difference between this breed and the Comet, except for coloration. The Tancho has a bright red cap and its body is usually silver or white. Pink can sometimes be found on the body or on the fins. The forked tail of a Tancho is also smaller than the Comet's.

The name Tancho comes from the Japanese word for "crane"; the Japanese crane also has a red spot on its head. *Tancho* can also be used to denote that type of coloration. Many fish in the carp family have Tancho coloration, including Koi.

Round or Egg-Shaped Body Type

The next two groups include some of the most exotic of all fish. They include a numbing variety of tails, body shapes, eye shapes, head shapes, and color combinations. You can see how a fascination with goldfish can easily last a lifetime.

As the name suggests, round or egg-shaped varieties look just like an egg with fins. They have short, rounded bodies, and it is difficult to distinguish head from body in some varieties.

Within the egg-shaped group, there are several varieties, such as the Lionhead and the Celestial, that lack a dorsal fin. The distinction here is very important. Goldfish that lack a dorsal fin do not swim as well as their cousins with dorsal fins. A Fantail, which has a dorsal fin, is a better swimmer than a Lionhead, which does not, and would be more likely to get the "lion's share" of the food. These are very important considerations when choosing goldfish.

It is important to know is that the fishes in this group, save the Fantail, the Ryunkin, and the Black Moor (depending on where you live), are not really suitable for most outdoor ponds or pools. They tend to need slightly warmer water, and some are not as hardy as the flat-bodied goldfish.

Dorsal-Finned Goldfish

This group tends to represent the moderate swimmers. They are faster than some more exotic varieties, but not as fast as their more streamlined cousins, such as the Comet. What this group lacks in streamlined form, it makes up in exaggerated fins and bright, bold colors.

The Fantail is one of the oldest varieties of Goldfish.

Fantail

Dating back some 1,300 to 1,500 years, the Fantail is one of the oldest goldfish varieties known. It is the most common fancy variety available to the average hobbyist. It is also the most popular, outselling all other fancy varieties.

This fish has a large double tail fin, which should be long and flowing. In the best Fantail specimens, the fish's tail should not be joined at any juncture along either side, but only at the caudal peduncle. The anal fins should be paired as well and, again, not joined in any place.

The most popular, most plentiful, and hardiest Fantails are solid orange metallic. The metallic orange color grows very deep and bright with age. Nacreous Fantails are also available, and those with the most blues and blacks are considered to be among the most prized. Nacreous Fantails are not as hardy as their orange metallic cousins.

This is one of the few fancy breeds that is durable and hardy enough for outdoor ponds. It is also the first fancy variety any hobbyist should own before moving into the more exotic breeds. With good care, a Fantail will grow to 3 to 6 inches in length, and has a life expectancy of somewhere between five and ten years.

This is a calico Ryunkin.

Nymph

These were popular for some time, but have fallen out of favor. It is thought that these goldfish are a cross between a Comet and a Fantail. The Nymph has a short body, is roundish with a deep belly and a short head, and has a large mouth with full lips and erect nostrils. It has extremely long fins and a dorsal fin that sits far back on the spine. Its pectoral and ventral fins are long, as is its single anal fin. The Nymph comes in single-tail, fantail, and fringe-tailed varieties.

Ryunkin

The Ryunkin is the Japanese version of the Fantail. Some argue that it is the older version of the Fantail. Legend has it that they were first developed on the Ryuku Islands, hence the name. The main difference between this variety and the Fantail is that this fish has a high, arching back, from which the dorsal fin extends even higher.

The back of the Ryunkin appears almost like a hump, which begins just after the head. Also, the tail is wider, meaning it is longer vertically instead of horizontally.

The Ryunkin can grow to between 3 and 6 inches and will live five to ten years. Ryunkins are available in all the color variations as the average Fantail, including Tancho. Ryunkins are excellent beginner fish for anyone wanting to

The Fishkeeper's Responsibilities

The fishkeeper (that's you) has an obligation to care for the fish that they have brought home. Because the fish are contained in an artificial environment, it is up to you to establish and to maintain their living space in an appropriate manner. The fishkeeper is responsible for providing:

- High water quality
- Proper feeding
- Correct water temperature
- A balanced fish community of the proper density
- Appropriate habitat and shelter
- Sufficient lighting

move toward keeping the more exotic breeds. They are also good for outdoor ponds or pools.

Veiltail

The origin of the Veiltail is under debate. Some claim that the Veiltail is actually a mutation of the Fantail, while others say the Veiltail was bred from the Wakin. Regardless of its ancestry, the Veiltail looks more like a Fantail.

The most striking feature of the Veiltail is its fins. The dorsal fin extends very high, usually straight up on a good specimen. All the other fins are long and extend downward in beautiful, flowing ribbons. The fish has a double caudal fin and the paired anal fins extend so far back that they are even with the middle of the elongated tail, which is not forked.

Although considered one of the most beautiful of all goldfish, Veiltails are not the hardiest. They are not the most delicate, either, but they do need more care than the average goldfish. Veiltails require space to swim because of their long fins, so the aquarium should not be overcrowded with other fish or too many plants. The quality of the water must be maintained so that they don't lose their color. Their fins are also very susceptible to rot and any number of fungal diseases.

The coloration of the Veiltail ranges from orange and red metallic to black to nacreous. The rounder and more ball-shaped the body, the better the specimen is thought to be.

Veiltails live four to six years and grow to 3 to 5 inches long, not including the length of the tail. They prefer to be kept in water somewhat warmer than the breeds already mentioned; don't let the water temperature drop to less than 50°F. Ideally, they should be kept between 65°F and 75°F.

Veiltails are not very competitive and should be kept only with other Veiltails. They are definitely for a more experienced hobbyist and will not tolerate pond or outdoor life.

Oranda

The Oranda is the result of crossing the Veiltail and the Lionhead. The body is egg-shaped and has long, flowing paired caudal and anal fins. The dorsal fin is very similar to that on a Veiltail. Some call this variety the Fantailed Lionhead because it looks as if it comes from Fantail stock, but this is a misnomer. In Japanese, it is called the *oranda shishigashira,* which means "rare Lionhead." The calico Oranda is called *azumanishiki.*

Like the Lionhead (one of those without a dorsal fin), the Oranda has a bumpy growth over its head that resembles a wart. On good specimens, this high head growth covers the head completely, like a cap. This growth, which begins to show at two to three years old, should not cover the eyes, nostrils, or mouth of the fish.

This Redcap Oranda shows an excellent growth on its head.

On the orange metallic Oranda, which is the most common, the head growth takes on a more concentrated orange color. On nacreous Orandas, the growth may be white, orange, red, yellow, black, blue, or calico. The more valuable Orandas have more blues and blacks. There is even a red cap, or Tancho, variety of Oranda, that is very striking and among the most highly prized, as its white body provides a stark contrast to the bright cherry-red cap that covers the head.

This fish has a life expectancy of approximately five to ten years, and should be kept at a relatively constant temperature of 65°F. Given enough room, an Oranda will grow to 3 to 4 inches, not including the length of the tail. Disease and fungus are sometimes a problem for Orandas, as these tend to develop in the folds and crevices of the cap. This fish should be kept only by someone who has experience with goldfish—it is definitely not for the beginner. Also, the Oranda is not right for a year-round outdoor pond.

Pearl-Scale

This is a variety that is growing in popularity. Essentially, it looks like a Fantail, except that it is shorter and fatter, somewhat like a Ryunkin, but with less exaggerated fins. Its back arches high and its dorsal fin begins just forward of what looks like a hunchback. The abdomen protrudes much more than on almost any of the egg-shaped breeds, making the body large and ball-like. The caudal fin can sometimes develop into square veiltails.

The Pearl-Scale's scales are spherical and have a raised area in the center.

The Pearl-Scale is known for its odd scales, which seem almost spherical because there is a hard, raised area in the center of each scale. These raised areas are usually white and look a bit like pearls sticking out of the fish's body. As you would imagine, fish with the larger scales are more greatly prized. An exceptional specimen exhibits these scales all the way up the body to the dorsal fin. When the scales fall off from rubbing, fights, or injury, they do grow back, but as flat, normal scales.

This fish has a life expectancy of approximately five to ten years, and should be kept at a relatively constant temperature between 49°F and 65°F, preferably toward the high end. Given enough room, a Pearl-Scale will grow to be the size of a baseball or bigger, not including the fins. Disease and fungus are sometimes a problem, as these tend to develop in the folds and crevices of the skin. Good aeration of the water is necessary to keep the fish healthy.

Telescope-Eyed or Globe-Eyed Goldfish

In Japanese, the word *demekin* means "goldfish with the protruding eyes." This variety has been known in China since the eighteenth century, where it was also known as the Dragon Fish or Dragon-Eyed Goldfish. In Britain it is known as the Pop-Eyed Goldfish. As the names clearly imply, the Globe-Eyed Goldfish is known for its eyes, which protrude in almost tubelike fashion up to three-quarters of an inch.

The eyes of this young Telescope-Eyed Goldfish will protrude even more as it grows.

In body type and finnage—a short, round, egg-shaped body with double anal and caudal fins—the Globe-Eyed Goldfish most resembles the Fantail. Coloration ranges from orange metallic to nacreous, with combinations similar to those usually found in Fantails. The Veiltail form of this variety is available, but the matte variation is extremely rare.

This fish lives about five to ten years and should be kept at a relatively constant temperature between 49°F and 65°F, leaning toward the warmer. Given enough room, a Globe-Eyed Goldfish will grow to 4 to 6 inches, tail length not included. Diseases and fungus are sometimes a problem, as the eyes are very delicate and sensitive.

The term "telescope" is quite misleading, because as these goldfish grow older (six months to a year), their eyes begin to protrude, thereby limiting their vision and putting them at a disadvantage. It is recommended that this fish be kept with its own kind or with other similarly handicapped fish. The Globe-Eyed Goldfish is definitely not for the beginner, and should be kept only by someone who has experience with goldfish. This goldfish variety is not suitable for ponds.

Black Moor

The Black Moor is basically a black variation of the Telescope-Eyed Goldfish. It is known for its velvetlike black coat. The telescoped eyes are a little larger and less prone to infection than the normal Telescope-Eyed Goldfish.

The Black Moor is basically a Telescope-Eyed Goldfish with larger eyes and a velvety black coat.

Other than the Fantail, the Black Moor is the only round or egg-shaped goldfish that is hardy enough to survive in outdoor ponds, depending on where you live. Consult your local aquarium store dealer. Like the Fantail, the Black Moor is a good goldfish for the beginner because it is so hardy.

The Black Moor has a life expectancy of approximately five to ten years, and should be kept at a relatively constant temperature between 49°F and 65°F, leaning toward the cooler. Given enough room, a Black Moor will grow to 4 to 6 inches, not including the length of the tail.

As Black Moors get older, they develop a velvety texture. However, if these fish are kept in water that is consistently too warm, orange will sometimes show through. Once this happens, there is usually no going back.

Dorsal-less Goldfish: The Exotics

Goldfish without dorsal fins (dorsal-less) are considered the worst swimmers of all the goldfish varieties. Without a dorsal fin, which keeps the fish right side up, it is difficult for them to swim quickly. Hence, they are not as fast, nor are they as quick to turn, as even the slow-moving Veiltail or Globe-Eyed Goldfish.

This group includes the most exotic of all the goldfish and, as a result, many of them are not recommended for beginners. These fish require care and maintenance from an experienced hobbyist. None of the fish in this final group is suitable for outdoor ponds or pools.

Ranchu

This is the simplest of all the Lionhead-type varieties. It is a roundish, egg-shaped fish with no dorsal fin. In Japan it is commonly called *maruko,* which means "round fish." This is a common name given to a number of fish, but the word seems most closely identified with this breed. Its back arches gracefully to the caudal peduncle, which points downward at approximately a 45-degree angle. The fins are usually short and include a dual caudal fin.

The most notable feature on this fish, however, is the head, which is covered with a type of cap or hood. Many goldfish experts liken the bumpy, fleshy covering, which is neither hard nor soft, to a raspberry. On most specimens, the cap doesn't begin to appear until their second year, growing until the fish is a little over three years old. Because the cap can impair the fish's breathing, the water in its tank must be well aerated.

The Japanese categorize three types of head growth: Tokin, which is just above the head resembling a cap; Okame, which covers the sides of the head with no growth on top, giving the impression of swollen or stuffed cheeks; and Shishigashira, which is a full hood covering the top of the head, the sides of the head, and the opercular areas (around the gill flaps).

All these goldfish come in metallic and nacreous forms, and color combinations of orange, red, yellow, silver, white, blue, violet, and black. As is typical of calico variations, the more blues and blacks, the more valuable the fish is thought to be.

This fish has a life expectancy of approximately five to ten years, and should be kept at a relatively constant temperature of 55°F to 65°F. Given enough room, a Ranchu will grow to 3 inches. Diseases such as fungus are sometimes a problem, as these develop in the folds and crevices of the cap. This fish should be kept only by someone who has experience with goldfish, and is definitely not for the beginner.

Lionhead

The Lionhead is the Chinese version of the Ranchu. It is the large, conspicuous hood that gives the fish its name, the fleshy cap resembling a lion's mane. The head growth tends to be more encompassing and much more pronounced. The Lionhead also tends to be larger, longer, and less streamlined than the Ranchu. This is because the Lionhead has a larger, broader back and head, and is sometimes thought to be boxier. The dual tail tends to be a little larger and more pronounced.

The Lionhead is much more popular in North America than the Ranchu. These fish are also known or marketed as Brambleheads, Buffalo-Heads, or Tomato-Heads.

These fish are not the best swimmers because of their body shape, and they tend to swim forward at a downward angle. Some experts attribute this to the lack of a dorsal fin, while others note the swim

This Lionhead has a calico pattern.

bladder location farther back, or the size of the cap. Regardless of the reason, this is not one of the more competitive goldfish, and therefore it should not be kept with active varieties such as Comets or Shubunkins. Even a Fantail is not a good companion for a Lionhead, regardless of size or age. You should ask your local aquarium dealer for advice on your mixture of goldfish.

You can expect the Lionhead to live approximately five to ten years. It should be kept at a relatively constant temperature between 55°F and 65°F. Given enough room, the Lionhead grows to 4 inches long. As is the case for most exotic varieties, diseases such as fungus are sometimes a problem. This fish should be kept only by an experienced hobbyist.

Marigold Chinese Lionhead

As the name suggests, this goldfish is a bright yellow variation of the Lionhead. The distinguishing feature of this goldfish, which is also known as Sunrise, is an extremely pronounced hood. It is so large that its yellow color makes it look very much like a marigold. They are extremely rare and usually are not available in commercial aquarium stores, but can be specially ordered. This variety is also more delicate than the ordinary Lionhead.

Pompon

The Pompon's body is short and boxy like a Lionhead, but the growth on the head is different. The Pompon's nasal septum (also known as narial flaps) is so enlarged that it grows outward into two tassels, or pompons, called narial bouquets—which are basically skin flaps folded over and over. These flaps, which have a velvety appearance, sway when the fish swims. This variety is also known as the Velvetball or the Velvetyball. As is typical of all growths on goldfish, these flaps can be susceptible to diseases, such as fungus. Older Pompons do develop Tokin, a caplike head growth similar to the Ranchu.

The most popular Pompon breed is of the orange dorsal-less type. However, there are also Pompon Orandas, Lionhead Pompons, and the Hanafusa, which is the dorsal-finned version of the same fish. These are not normally available to the average consumer.

Pompons come in metallic and nacreous forms, and are seen in combinations of orange, red, yellow, silver, white, blue, violet, and black. In calico variations, the more blues and blacks, the more valuable the fish is thought to be. This goldfish lives approximately five to ten years, and should be kept at 55°F to 65°F. With enough room, Pompons grow to 4 inches.

Brocaded Goldfish

Known as Kinranshi in Japan, this goldfish is thought to be a cross between the Lionhead and the Ryunkin. The body resembles that of the Wakin, while the finnage, especially the lack of a dorsal fin, reminds one of a Lionhead. Its coloration includes rich gold mottled with black, red, and white, just like gold brocade. It was first bred in Japan in 1905 by Akiyama Kichigoro.

Celestial

The Celestial goldfish is believed by some experts to have been developed in Korea in the late 1700s, and was not bred in Japan or China until after the turn of the twentieth century. However, other experts say this fish, which the Chinese named Stargazer, was bred in China first. Regardless, the Japanese call it

Demeranchu and it is also known by the names Chiutien, Ngarn, and Chotengan.

The Celestial is so named because its eyes point skyward, positioned on top of outgrowths, rather than at the ends. This growth begins at a very early age. Since the eyes of these goldfish are directed upward, their forward and lateral vision is poor and they tend to feel their way around or position themselves to see. In a good specimen, the fish's eyes are pointed in the same direction and the pupils are the same size.

The Celestial is somewhat more streamlined than the other dorsal-less goldfish, but it still most closely resembles the Lionhead and the Ranchu. Celestial goldfish come in metallic and nacreous forms, and are seen in combinations of orange, red, yellow, silver, white, blue, violet, and black. As is typical of calico variations, the more valuable fish have more blues and blacks.

Celestials should be kept at a relatively constant temperature between 55°F and 65°F, and have a life expectancy of approximately five to ten years. Given enough room, the Celestial goldfish will grow to 6 inches. Again, diseases such as fungus are sometimes a problem, as the eyes are very delicate and sensitive.

Bubble-Eye

These goldfish are known for the large, fluid-filled sacs that grow beneath each eye. The eye itself is quite normal, but in almost half these fish, the sacs grow so

The reason for the Bubble-Eye's name is obvious.

tight and large that the eyes begin to point upward like those of a Celestial. The sacs, which should always be of the same size, are very delicate and prone to injury, but they do heal. When the fish swims, these sacs bounce, giving it a precarious look.

The Bubble-Eye has a body like a Celestial, which is slightly sleeker than the Lionhead or the Ranchu, but nothing like that of the Comet or the Common Goldfish. It has a dual caudal fin and is dorsal-less. Unlike the Pompon, the Ranchu, and the Lionhead, it develops no other growth on the head at any time.

These fish come in metallic and nacreous forms, and are seen in combinations of red, orange, yellow, silver, white, blue, violet, and black. The more blues and blacks in the calico variations, the more valuable the fish.

This fish can live for up to ten years and should be kept at 55°F to 65°F. The Bubble-Eye goldfish will grow to 5 inches, given adequate room. Diseases are sometimes a problem, as the eyes are very delicate and sensitive. All sharp objects should be removed from the tank to avoid injuring this fish. The Bubble-Eye needs expert care.

Black Bubble-Eye

Another fancy species, the Black Bubble-Eye, is a black, velvety version of the Bubble-Eye. The information about the Bubble-Eye applies to this fish.

Egg Fish

This is an appropriately named fish, because it looks like an egg with fins. With a short, round, egg-shaped body, the Egg Fish lacks a dorsal fin but has a large fantail and large pectoral and pelvic fins. This is a very popular fish in China and was a popular goldfish in the United States and Britain for some time. It has now fallen out of favor and is difficult to find.

It is most commonly found in metallic-orange and calico colorations. A black version of this fish has also been bred, but is extremely rare.

Meteor

This is one of the strangest and most exotic of all goldfish because it lacks something that all other goldfish have: a tail. With its round shape, the Meteor has a high, erect dorsal fin and a large anal fin, both of which make up for the missing caudal fin. Meteors are very rare. However, the growing interest in this breed will likely bring them more notoriety—and availability.

Chapter 3

Choosing Your Goldfish

Keep in mind that all goldfish have been bred from the common goldfish, *Carassius auratus*. All goldfish are basically a variation on two or three body types. There are the sleeker fish, like the Comet; egg-shaped goldfish, like the Pearl-Scale; and egg-shaped goldfish without dorsal fins, like the Ranchu. Basically, all the varieties have at one time or another been bred with all the other varieties, creating one more variety for each new fish. This may make it tempting to mix different types of goldfish in the same tank.

The only real way to keep goldfish with other goldfish is to keep the same types together in groups. For example, Comets and Bubble-Eyes would not live comfortably together, because the former swim faster and tend to eat more and faster than the latter, which are delicate and need expert handling.

Like all fish, goldfish tend to pick on injured or much smaller fish, especially if the aquarium is crowded. Generally speaking, though, goldfish are not aggressive when kept with other goldfish of the same type. They do tend to be aggressive during breeding time. However, males do not fight for the right to mate with a female goldfish. Instead, male goldfish chase the females until they eventually get their chance to spawn.

Goldfish and Other Tropical Fish

When you are choosing goldfish, any good aquarium dealer will tell you that this species should not be kept with other tropical fish. Goldfish should be kept with goldfish. Why? There are many reasons.

> In ponds or pools, goldfish tend to school. In these schools, there is never a lead goldfish—the school merely darts around following one fish or another.

Overall, goldfish are hardier than other tropical fish. They do not require a heater in their tank, and are actually better off if the temperature gets cold for a little while (six to eight weeks each year). Tropical fish, for the most part, require a consistent temperature in the low 70s, while goldfish can live comfortably in the mid- to low 40s. Although goldfish can certainly survive in higher temperatures, they tend to be more susceptible to disease when they're too warm.

Goldfish don't really get along with other fish, either. Depending on the variety, goldfish can be too aggressive or they can end up as the other fish's lunch. Goldfish might also become territorial when kept with some kinds of common community fish. For example, angelfish and goldfish don't get along. Kept with cichlids, such as Oscars and Jack Dempseys, your goldfish is likely to be gone by morning.

Finally, given the opportunity, goldfish will grow significantly larger than many other aquarium fish. Of course, there are exceptions among the tropical

Keep similar varieties of goldfish together in the same tank, and don't mix them in with other species.

fish world, including the Oscar and the Arrowana—both of which feed on small fish, including goldfish.

Another thing to remember is never to place Perch, Sunfish, or any other natural wildlife in with your goldfish. Although these are also cold-water fish, they are generally more aggressive and hardier than goldfish. Some will also eat goldfish.

Keeping the Bottom of the Tank Clean

If you're wondering if you need a catfish to keep the bottom of your tank clean, the short answer is no. Goldfish are excellent bottom feeders, constantly scouting the aquarium floor for available food. In the end, goldfish will do the job themselves. Besides, many tropical catfish are not able to withstand the colder temperatures that goldfish prefer.

Signs of a Healthy Goldfish

Regardless of the variety, there are telltale signs you should look for when selecting your fish. Look at your prospective fish very carefully, because you do not want to buy an unhealthy fish right from the start.

- **Activity level.** This is the most important thing to look for. You want healthy, active fish that swim smoothly and seem alert to their surroundings. Do not buy a fish that is spending all its time at the top or at the bottom of the tank, that is swimming on its side, or that is upside-down. Avoid any fish that looks as if it's having trouble swimming.
- **Eyes.** Never let a dealer sell you a fish that has cloudy eyes, cataracts, or any other kind of malady of the eyes, unless that person is an expert in that breed. A goldfish's eyes should be bright and clear, and the fish should react to light.
- **Fins.** All the goldfish's fins, including the caudal fin, should be erect or upright and intact. You should not buy a fish with spots anywhere on its fins, and there should be no frayed, split, or folded surfaces.
- **Scales.** If there are any signs of fungus, white or otherwise, any wounds, or any missing scales, don't buy the fish. Fish should have unblemished bodies with no missing scales and no hint of disease.

Select the healthiest fish to bring home for your aquarium.

Avoid Overcrowding

Goldfish are very hardy fish. They are generally very active and are capable of growing quite large. The common goldfish can grow to more than a foot! The general rule is 1 inch of fish for each gallon of water your aquarium tank will hold. But you can't keep a 12-inch goldfish in a 12-gallon tank. When selecting the number of goldfish you want, be sure to keep in mind the size of your aquarium (see the box on page 43).

Overcrowding will create poor water quality and your fish will suffer. You simply cannot supply enough oxygen to accommodate an overcrowded aquarium. The idea is to create an environment that is beneficial to the fish, not to pack as many fish into as small a place as possible. The more space per goldfish, the healthier and more active they will be.

How to Avoid Overcrowding

Overcrowding is not good for your goldfish, your aquarium, or your nerves. It is important to keep the number of fish in balance with the number of gallons of water in your tank. Use this information as a guide when setting up your aquarium.

Gallons of Water	Number of Goldfish
1	1
5	2–3
10	3–4
20	6–8
30	9–12

Part II
Goldfish Habitats

Chapter 4

Setting Up Your Aquarium

There is no more popular image of the goldfish than one living in a goldfish bowl. However, a goldfish bowl is no more an aquarium than a closet is a home. While goldfish are extremely easy to care for, one of the things they absolutely need is well-aerated water.

The water in a goldfish bowl is not well aerated because the typical goldfish bowl is wide in the middle and narrow on top. What you need is an aquarium or container with a wide top for maximum exposure to air. The more water surface that is exposed to air, the more oxygen and gas exchange, resulting in enough air for your goldfish to breathe comfortably.

For anyone who has seen a goldfish in a bowl, the one thing you probably remember is seeing the goldfish breathing rather heavily near the surface of the water. This is because the goldfish was suffocating. The oxygen in the water had been quickly used up, leaving the fish no choice but to hang near the surface and gulp for air. This is not good for your fish.

Also, a Common Goldfish grows to be 10 to 14 inches long—but not in a bowl. You generally need one gallon of water for every inch of adult goldfish (see chapter 3 for more on tank capacity), unless you are intentionally trying to dwarf your fish. What your goldfish needs is an aquarium.

Aquarium Tanks

Most tanks today are either made of glass sealed with silicone, or they are acrylic. If you buy a glass aquarium, make sure the tank does not have any scratches or seams that are not caulked with the silicone cement. Such tanks will have a tendency either to leak or to burst.

The first thing you need to remember when placing your tank on any surface is that it will be filled with water—and water is *heavy!* Water weighs approximately 8 pounds per gallon. A 10-gallon tank weighs approximately 80 pounds and a 20-gallon tank would be approximately 160 pounds, and this doesn't include the weight of the gravel, filter, and other fixtures. It is important that you use the strongest piece of furniture possible—or make your life simple and buy an aquarium stand from your local aquarium supply store.

Surface Area

Buy an aquarium that will offer the greatest amount of surface area. Surface area is the amount of space exposed to air at the top of the tank. For example, a deep 20-gallon tank will offer less surface area than a long 20-gallon tank. You therefore don't want to choose a deep tank, because the water won't be well aerated. It will also be difficult to adjust equipment and to clean. Besides, goldfish would rather swim farther than deeper.

Keep in mind that the better aerated the water, the more fish you can comfortably house. A longer tank, with more surface area, offers you the option of supporting more fish. Maybe only one or two extra, but that certainly is a big value to the beginner.

Cover or Hood

After you have chosen your tank, you need to buy a cover (or hood) and a light. The cover performs a number of functions:

- It stops unwanted objects from entering the tank and possibly injuring the fish.
- It stops the fish from jumping out of the tank, as they sometimes do. This, of course, can be fatal if no one is around to find them and return them to the water.
- It stops splashes from affecting your carpeting, your hardwood floor, and your furniture.
- It keeps the water from damaging the light over the tank.
- It cuts down on evaporation.

The hood is generally fitted to the dimensions of the tank and is adjustable to allow for aquarium accessories. It should be composed of thick ($1/8$-inch) glass

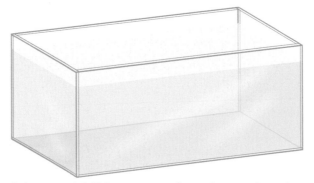

Even though these two tanks hold the same amount of water, the rectangular one has a much larger surface area at the top and the water will be better aerated.

or plastic, so it can support the weight of other aquarium components, if necessary. It should be segmented so the entire assembly need not be removed to feed the fish or work in the tank.

For the beginner, I strongly recommend the type of hood that also contains the aquarium light. These units are self-contained and are designed to keep water away from the lighting unit, to minimize danger, and to cover the entire tank. If possible, the tank, stand, and hood should be purchased as a package from a single manufacturer. This prevents the problem of mismatched aquarium components, and may also be less expensive.

Where to Put the Aquarium?

Before you choose an aquarium, first consider where you are going to keep it. Think about that first, because the size of the tank you buy must fit in the spot you have chosen. Whichever room you choose, never place the tank in front of a window. The result will be algae—and lots of it. While light is necessary, placing the tank in front of a window will make for cleaning chores of the worst kind. You also need to choose a location that has an adequate electrical supply and is not too far from a source of water.

Well-used living areas are excellent settings for aquariums, because the fish acclimate to people entering and leaving the room. Placing the aquarium in a rarely used area will leave you with fish that are skittish and timid when people approach.

Finally, choose a location that can tolerate a water spill. Even the most meticulous of aquarists spill water around an aquarium, and in many cases water is splashed from a tank.

Remember, once you set a tank up, you can't move it.

Light

Lighting is necessary both for illumination and to promote plant growth. Many aquarium lights are fluorescent. These provide even, cool lighting and use less energy than incandescent lights. Although incandescent lights offer good, strong lighting for plants, they do produce heat and tend to be more expensive to run. Whether you choose fluorescent or incandescent, make sure that you get a white, natural, or daylight-grade colored light.

Your aquarium supply dealer carries a full variety of fluorescent lightbulbs. If you buy your fish tank with a hood and light canopy (as I recommend), it will most likely have a fluorescent light. If you do not buy a tank, cover, and light package, make sure the light you buy extends across the entire length of the tank. This is by far the most efficient and economical form of lighting available for your tank, and I thoroughly recommend it.

Your fish and plants need light, but only for half the day. Make sure you get a timer so the light goes off and your fish can rest.

When choosing your lighting, consider the depth of your aquarium and the number of live plants you intend to grow. These two aspects of your tank dictate the power, number, and type of bulbs you buy. The general rule is 2 to 2.5 watts per gallon of water. A 10-gallon tank would then require 20 to 25 watts of light.

An often-overlooked component to the lighting system is an on-off timer switch. Goldfish need their rest! A timer switch automatically turns on and shuts off your lighting system so that a consistent day length can be maintained. A twelve-hour day length is generally recommended for most aquariums.

You should always try not to startle your fish, so avoid suddenly switching the light on or off. To better simulate a normal sunset, switch off the aquarium light about an hour before other room lights are turned off. This little detail will help keep your fish happy and well adjusted.

Heater

Welcome to the world of the cold-water aquarist. Because you have goldfish, you do not absolutely need to have an aquarium heater. The hardier strains of goldfish can generally withstand temperatures almost down to freezing. Some of the other varieties are less hardy, but can easily withstand temperatures in the low 60s.

As long as you live in a warm climate or have heating in your home all day and night, there is normally no need for a heater in your aquarium. However, the smaller the tank, the more quickly the temperature may change. This is why many goldfish keepers have heaters. Having a heater in the tank is a wise precaution. It will keep your aquarium at a constant temperature and make your life a little easier.

There are a few types of aquarium heaters available, but the most common is a submersible glass tube with a built-in thermostat. This heater attaches to the side of the tank and has external controls. Once it is properly set, it automatically responds to changes in water temperature and turns on and off. An indicator light usually lets you know that the heater is on. The fully submersible heater, which can be placed completely in the tank, also responds automatically to changes in water temperature.

In general, you should place your heater close to an area of high water circulation so that heated water can be rapidly and evenly distributed throughout the tank. This is usually near the filter system or the airstones.

Never pull your heater out of the water while it is on, because this is a good way to ruin your thermostat and possibly crack the glass housing—and you can get hurt. Remember, water and electricity do not mix.

How Much Power?

Heaters come in a variety of sizes; buy one that is matched to the size of your tank. Just like aquarium lights, you buy heaters by wattage. The basic rule is 5 watts for every gallon of water. A 10-gallon tank therefore requires a 50-watt heater, a 20-gallon tank requires a 100-watt heater, a 30-gallon tank calls for a 150-watt heater, and so on.

When you get to 30 gallons and beyond, it's a good idea to split the wattage between two heaters, placing one at either end of the tank, to ensure that the water is evenly heated. Therefore, for a 30-gallon tank, you need two 75-watt heaters.

Don't Forget a Thermometer

Even though your heater has a thermostat, you still need a thermometer to monitor the temperature of the water and to properly set the heater. There are two types of thermometers that are popular. The first is the internal floating thermometer, which, as the term implies, floats freely in the aquarium. The second is the external thermometer that you stick on the outside of the tank. The

You can buy aquarium setups that include all the equipment you'll need. These are fancy ones, but there are more basic models.

external thermometers tend to read a bit low—about 2°F lower than the actual water temperature—so keep that in mind.

Water Filters

There are three basic types of filters for the average goldfish aquarium: box filters, which go inside the tank; power filters, which go outside the tank; and undergravel filters, which go in the tank, under the gravel (of course!). The first two have layers of filter floss and charcoal to remove debris and chemicals from the water, while the undergravel filter uses the gravel as a natural filter.

Before we get into the specifics of each type of filter, let's discuss what a water filter does in your aquarium. A filter has two or three purposes, depending on which kind you use. First, it cleanses and purifies the water. Second, it circulates the water. Third, in most cases it aerates the water.

I recommend an external power filter for most beginner aquariums. If your tank is 10 gallons or larger and you want to keep goldfish, you really must use one. External power filters are easy to maintain and they clean more water faster than any of the other filter types. This is important, because goldfish are not the neatest of fish and you need a strong filter to keep their water clean and healthy.

Even if you keep just one fish in a small tank, you need to provide filtration.

Goldfish are too messy and too active for a box filter, which will not provide enough air, or an undergravel filter, which will not be strong enough to sift out all the debris—of which goldfish seem to create an endless supply.

However, if you are keeping *just one very small* goldfish in a tank that is smaller than 10 gallons, you still really need to provide some kind of filtration. In that case, a small box filter or an undergravel filter may be sufficient, so I will describe them here.

Box Filter

Known also as an inside, corner, or bottom filter, the box filter is the simplest of all filters. It's usually shaped like a cube and is packed with a layer charcoal sandwiched between two layers of fibrous material (filter floss). This series of layers is sometimes collectively known as a mat. The mat should be tamped down but not too tightly packed. The materials should be loose enough for water to flow through easily.

The layers of fibrous material sift out debris, providing what is called mechanical filtration. These layers also house bacteria that convert toxic substances to less toxic compounds; this is called biological filtration. The layer of charcoal purifies the water, taking out any toxic materials and providing chemical filtration.

Air, driven by an air pump, flows down a tube and creates water flow through the box filter. The air pump sits outside the tank and must be plugged into a wall socket. Finding a quiet, powerful pump is important with any filtration device. The more powerful the air pump, the more effectively the filter operates and the better aerated the water.

Undergravel Filters

Biologically speaking, the undergravel filter was once considered one of the best filters. Placed on the bottom of the tank before anything else, this simple filter is basically a perforated plastic plate. Gravel, plants, and all other tank fixtures are placed on top of the filter, and the gravel acts as the filter media. Air is pumped down to airstones in two plastic tubes on either side of the filter, thereby drawing water through the gravel and out the tubes. In advanced models, water is pulled through the gravel by small pumps, called powerheads, mounted on each tube.

The undergravel filter uses helpful bacteria to biologically filter the aquarium. It usually takes several weeks to establish the bacterial population, but then this filter is very efficient. Uneaten food, fish waste, and other substances in aquarium decay into ammonia, which is not good for fish. As water passes through the gravel, the bacteria convert the ammonia into nitrites and then into nitrates. The fish can live with nitrates.

For goldfish, it is important to place enough gravel in the tank that the fish do not dig so deep into the gravel that they disturb the bacterial population you are trying so hard to establish. Since goldfish are such good bottom feeders and gravel movers, they sometimes make this type of filtration difficult—which is why I don't really recommend it.

If you have live plants, this system is both a blessing and a curse. The nitrates produced by the bacteria provide fertilizer for your plants, helping them to thrive. However, because of the way the undergravel filter works, the filtering process wreaks havoc on the plants' root systems, ruining their chances of survival. To solve this problem, you can terrace the gravel in one area and place most of the plants there. In the terraced area, your plants will meet with less turbulence from the filter system.

External Power Filters

The external power filter is the easiest and least complicated filter system for the beginner's aquarium. These filters are specifically designed to turn over large amounts of water. The external power filter hangs on the side of the tank and is powered by its own motor. Water is drawn into the filter through a U-shaped siphon tube. It passes over layers of fibrous filter material and activated carbon and is returned to the tank via a gravity trickle system or a return pipe. Like the box filter, the power filter also circulates the water, providing aeration.

While it works on the same premise as the box filter, the power filter is much more efficient at removing waste and debris from the tank. It does not need to be cleaned as frequently as the box filter. Many models have special filter cartridges that make cleaning these filters extremely easy. In addition, various types of cartridges can be purchased to chemically alter water quality and correct water chemistry problems.

The external canister filter is the next step up in power filters. This filter is much larger than the others and is designed to filter large tanks of 50 gallons or more. The canister filter is composed of a large jarlike canister, which generally sits next to the tank. It contains filter media and activated carbon, like the other filters, but has a much more powerful motor for filtering large amounts of water. Water is drawn up by an intake suction line and sent back to the aquarium through a return line. If the return line is properly positioned, these filters can provide water circulation. I recommend this kind of filter for the aquarist with a larger tank.

Goldfish tend to be messy, so make sure you provide adequate filtration.

Aeration

Goldfish need a lot of oxygen. An air pump increases circulation in the tank, promotes oxygen exchange at the surface, and increases the escape of carbon dioxide, carbon monoxide, and free ammonia from the tank. This increase in circulation also acts to mix all the aquarium levels so that a uniform temperature is maintained throughout the tank.

Although most filters provide water circulation and aeration, it is a very good idea to have an external air pump moving air through one or more airstones in the tank. The more oxygen in the tank, the more goldfish you will be able to house comfortably, within reason. Having an airstone or some other device that releases air into the water can generally raise the number of fish you can support by about two for a 10-gallon tank, three for a 20-gallon tank, and four for a 30-gallon tank.

Air Pump

The size of your air pump depends on the type of filter you choose. If you have an external power filter or a canister filter, you need only a small pump to supply more oxygen to the water through an airstone or other aeration device. If you choose a box or an undergravel filter, you will want a more powerful pump so you can easily operate those devices as well as an airstone.

Air pumps are left on 24 hours a day. They are never shut off, except when you are dismantling the filters or the tank for cleaning.

There are two basic kinds of pumps: diaphragm pumps, which have a vibrating rubber diaphragm, and piston pumps. Both are good additions to any aquarium. While the diaphragm type requires no attention, piston pumps do require occasional oiling. Piston pumps tend to deliver more power, though. Pumps are made in many sizes to support anything from a large bowl to a group of several tanks. Talk to your aquarium supply professional about how much power you'll need for your setup.

Airstones

An airstone, which is generally made of porous rock, is attached to the air pump by an air hose. The stone splits the airstream into tiny bubbles, which aerate the water. You don't want too fine a mist, which will cause the bubbles to stick to various tank decorations and to the fish. Other aerators, like sunken treasure chests, fallen barrels, and old-fashioned underwater divers, are usually made of plastic or ceramic.

Aerators come in all kinds of attractive styles. Make sure the bubbles are not too fine, or they will just stick to your fish and will not aerate the water.

Remember, you don't want big bubbles racing to the surface. You want a steady stream of medium-sized bubbles that take their time going upward, causing water movement and aerating the water.

I strongly recommend that you have at least one airstone in a 10- or 20-gallon tank, and at least two in a 30-gallon tank or larger.

Air Hose

Your air pump and airstones require an air hose to link the two. This is plastic tubing that delivers air from your pump to the airstone. It should fit snugly at all joints so air does not escape from the system. Air leaks reduce the efficiency of the system (filter and airstone) and may ultimately burn out the pump. Make sure the tubing is manufactured for use in an aquarium; other grades may be toxic to fish.

Air Valves

If you intend to run multiple airstones or additional devices, such as filters, from a single pump, you need one or more air valves. These enable airflow to be directed to several devices from a single pump. They also enable you to control the airflow to these different devices. Using several air valves lets you turn devices on and off as you like. If you intend to do this, the pump should be big enough to supply air to all your devices.

Other Accessories

There are several other things you'll need, and a few you might like to have.

Algae Sponge or Aquarium Cleaner

An algae sponge or aquarium cleaner is a sponge attached to a long handle that is used for scraping down the inside of the tank. The sponge easily scrapes off algae but does not scratch the tank. A magnetic aquarium cleaner is also an effective cleaning tool. This uses two magnets with attached cleaning surfaces. One magnet is kept outside the tank and the other is controlled by the outside magnet to clean the inside walls.

An algae sponge attached to a long handle will help you keep the tank clean.

Aquarium Backdrop

Although not an essential piece of equipment, many aquarists like to have an aquarium backdrop. It's a paper or plastic backing that you place on the outside of the back wall of the aquarium. This conceals tubes, filters, pumps, and other fixtures that are usually kept behind the tank. Since many tanks are placed against the wall, the backdrop prevents you from seeing the paint or wallpaper on the wall behind the tank, as well. Aquarium backdrops come in a variety of colors, shades, and scenes. Choose one that you find most appealing and that fits the decor of your aquarium.

Your tank decorations can be natural or unnatural. Your fish will not care, as long as everything is safe and nontoxic.

Aquarium Vacuum

An aquarium vacuum is a must for the beginner. This is usually a hand pump siphon that enables you to extract larger debris from the aquarium floor without having to submerge your hands or use a net. This is especially helpful with goldfish, which are so messy. Regular vacuuming takes care of the very necessary task of cleaning your tank to maintain a debris-free environment.

Bucket and Hose

Set aside a 5-gallon bucket and a siphon hose for your aquarium. Then you will not have to prepare a clean bucket and hose every time you need one, and it will reduce the likelihood of introducing toxic agents into the aquarium (which is much more likely if you use a different bucket or hose each time).

> ### TIP
>
> Before you buy the decorative components of your tank, take the time to sketch out on paper just how you want your aquarium to look. Once you have a conceptual design in mind and on paper, setting up your aquarium will be much easier.

Decorations

Aquarium supply stores sell a variety of tank decorations that enhance the habitat for your fish. Some are plastic or ceramic creations and others are simply attractive rocks and stones. By buying these tank decorations from a dealer, you avoid contaminating your tank with toxic substances and agents that may modify your water chemistry. Avoid the temptation to collect your own rocks until you know how to identify each kind and understand its influence on your aquarium.

Before buying any decorations for your aquarium, take the time to design the kind of setting you want to build for your fish. In their natural habitat, fish have access to shelter as well as sufficient swimming space. Caves and rock ledges mimic your fish's natural habitat and increase their sense of security and well-being.

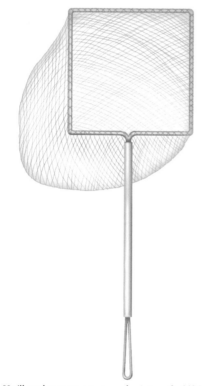

Fishnets

You will definitely need a fishnet or two. It's better to have a couple of sizes handy, depending on the size of your tank and the size of your goldfish. Too small a net does not enable you to corner a fish, and too large a net is difficult to maneuver in the tank. You'll use a fishnet more than you think. It comes in very handy when you need to remove a fish that is ill or dead, or an aggressive fish, or when the time has come to clean the tank and remove all the fish.

Gravel

Gravel is an important component when setting up any fish tank, and this is especially so with goldfish, which are excellent scavengers and bottom feeders. Gravel is a natural

You'll need as many nets as you have sizes of goldfish.   addition that provides anchorage for plants and other decorations and also provides a home for useful bacteria that power the nitrogen cycle and rid the aquarium of toxic wastes.

If Your Goldfish Gets Gravel Stuck in Its Mouth

Goldfish sometimes get bits of gravel caught in their mouths. In most cases, they will dislodge the gravel over several hours without damage to the fish. However, if the gravel does not dislodge, attempt the following, which is recommended by the Goldfish Society of America in its *Official Guide to the Goldfish:*

1. Capture the fish with a fishnet.
2. Hold the fish head down and press against both sides of the lips, opening its mouth.
3. Press the throat with your other fingers. Relief is usually immediate.

I thoroughly recommend against collecting gravel or aquarium decorations from the wild. Rather, buy them from an aquarium supply dealer. Certain kinds of materials can alter the chemistry of the aquarium, creating water hardness problems. The items you buy are also guaranteed to be nontoxic and clean.

Gravel comes in a variety of sizes, ranging from coarse to very fine. Goldfish routinely take up big bunches of gravel, hold them in their mouths, and then spit them back out. Goldfish are also known for moving gravel around, sometimes making a mess of your aquascaping. The gravel should therefore not be so fine as to be accidentally ingested, and it should be smooth so that it does not damage the fishes' mouths.

Medium pea-size gravel is a good choice. Gravel also comes in a variety of colors, ranging from bright reds to natural tones of gray. This decision is based solely on your taste, but be mindful of the color of your lighting when choosing your gravel colors.

The gravel should be about 1.5 to 2 inches deep on the aquarium bottom. If you use an undergravel filter, 2.5 to 3 inches is recommended. It is always best to buy a bit extra, so that when you aquascape your tank, you have enough to shape the bottom.

Water Quality Test Kits

Later in this chapter, I will describe how you use these to establish a healthy environment in your tank. Make sure when you buy your complete aquarium

To keep your fish and tank healthy, you'll need to test the water periodically.

setup that these are not left out. Test kits that measure pH, hardness, and nitrogen compounds are a must. The nitrogen kits should include tests for ammonia, nitrite, and nitrate.

Setting Up Your Aquarium

The first step in properly setting up your new aquarium is to assemble all the components in the area where you want the aquarium to be. Inventory the various components of the aquarium system and make sure that you are not missing any essential equipment.

Once you are confident that everything is in order, follow these steps to set up your aquarium.

1. Make sure everything is clean. Give the gravel, tank, filter, heater, aquarium decorations, artificial plants, and anything else you expect to put in the tank a thorough rinsing with clean, warm water. Do not use soap of any kind; soap can cause immediate water-quality problems. Start with the gravel: Empty it into a container, fill it up with water, swash it all about, dump the water, and start all over again. Agitate the gravel during each

rinse to get the dirt and other debris off it. Generally, for brand-new gravel, four or five thorough rinsings are enough. Don't skimp on this step, as dirty gravel will not only make cloudy water, but the water will be unsafe for your goldfish.

2. Place the tank on its stand exactly where you want it to be. Do not expect to move the tank once it is filled with water! Pour the gravel gently into the tank and begin the aquascaping of your tank. Terrace the gravel so that it is low in front and high toward the back of the tank.

3. Add any large pieces or decorations—rocks, pieces of wood, and so on. All these should also be thoroughly rinsed off before being placed into the tank. Use a clean, new scrubbing brush to remove dirt. Again, don't use soap—just clean water. Don't attempt to add plants (either real or artificial) or smaller decorations until the water is added to the tank because they may be displaced by the filling process. Remember to leave spaces for heaters, filters, and other equipment.

4. Add the airstones to the aquarium, taking the opportunity to conceal the air supply tubing behind larger decorations.

5. Add tap water to the tank. The container to carry water from the tap to the aquarium should be free of any soap (use your 5-gallon aquarium bucket). To avoid disrupting your aquascape, place a clean plate or bowl on the substrate and pour the water onto it. After water is added, you may need to touch up your aquascape.

6. Place the filter and heater in the tank and position them. Prepare the filter by following the manufacturer's instructions regarding filter media before setting it on or in the tank. Position the heater in a way that maximizes its output—near sources of water circulation such as filter outlets or airstones.

7. Place the smaller decorations in the tank, add the thermometer, and fine-tune your aquascape. Add any artificial or live plants. If you are using live plants, remember to weigh them down until root systems are well established.

8. Fit the hood, making sure the external components and electrical equipment are properly placed. Add the light on top of the canopy and make sure it is connected correctly.

9. Hook up all the hoses. When you are confident that the electrical wiring is safely insulated from sources of water, plug the aquarium units in and turn on the system. Make sure the heater is properly adjusted; this may take a day or so. Check the operation of the filter, air pumps, and light.

10. Let the tank water mature before adding any fish.

Don't place the fish in the tank immediately. Wait at least forty-eight hours because the water needs to stabilize. You also want to make sure that the tank is running properly before putting in the fish.

Water circulation, temperature regulation, and filtration will help your water stabilize in a relatively short time. Some experts would have you wait as long as two weeks, but I think that's too long for any enthusiastic hobbyist. Keep in mind that goldfish are a fairly hardy species.

Aquascaping

In general, aquascaping means setting up the inside of the tank so that it is pleasing to the human eye as well as pleasing to the fish. Aquascaping includes the placement of rocks, airstones, plants, and any other decorative pieces you've decided to include. The concept is to set up something resembling a natural habitat.

Some people make a rough sketch or find a photograph of how they would like their aquarium to look. It is advisable to have a good idea of what you want before you go into the store. If you decide to use an aquarium background, you

Have a clear sense of how you want to aquascape your tank before you start putting things in it.

may want to blend this with your aquascaping. Don't place too many objects in the tank—don't overaquascape. Make sure to leave plenty of space for your goldfish to swim. Fish also like to have places to hide, especially in plants.

Place the smaller plants and objects up front. Depending on the plants you choose, some will need to be bunched together while others need to stand alone. It is usually best to leave plenty of open space up front, so that you can view the fish when they are most active.

Rocks and wood are best when purchased at aquarium supply stores, so as to avoid any problems with toxicity that might hurt your fish. If you must use rocks from around your home, it is a good idea to boil them first. Land rocks are not as good as rocks taken from ponds because they may leach toxic compounds. Of all rocks, shale and slate tend to be the best because they do not contain a lot of impurities. Driftwood is a nice touch, but make sure to have driftwood that is weighted down. It is best to buy this from an aquarium supply store, so that it is guaranteed to be properly cured for your goldfish.

The Water

Goldfish are freshwater, coldwater fish—rather hardy animals. Even the exotic goldfish are pretty hardy where water is concerned. However, there are a few water-quality parameters

> **CAUTION**
>
> Never place seashells or any marine life in with your goldfish. These are not freshwater items and will cause the water to become much too alkaline for your fish.

that you must be aware of: water hardness, pH, and nitrogen. Before you place your goldfish in the aquarium, make sure to test the water.

Hardness

The amount of dissolved mineral salts—that is, calcium and magnesium—in the water is referred to as its hardness. Water with high concentrations of salts is called "hard," while low levels create "soft" water. The degree of hardness scale (dH) ranges from 0 to more than 30 degrees, with 4 to 8 degrees being soft water and 18 to 30 degrees being hard water.

Goldfish do best in water between 3 and 14 degrees of hardness. While goldfish can survive hard water, there is no need to place your fish at risk. The beginner generally does not need to alter water hardness unless the local tap water is excessively hard or soft. Commercial kits are now available to test and alter the degree of water hardness. These can be purchased at an aquarium supply store.

Your aquarium supply dealer will be able to tell you a great deal about your local water supply and what test kits and water treatments you may need.

pH

When we talk about pH, we are really referring to levels of hydrogen ions in solution. Ions are simply atoms with an electrical charge. These hydrogen ions have a positive charge. We measure the number of hydrogen ions on a pH scale.

The pH scale tells us how many hydrogen ions are in your aquarium water and, therefore, how acidic it is. It ranges from 0 to 14. While you would anticipate that a higher number on the scale would mean more hydrogen ions and a more acidic solution, this is not the case. In reality, the lower number on the scale means more hydrogen ions. A pH of 1 is very acidic, a pH of 7 is neutral, and a pH of 14 is very alkaline, which is the opposite of acidic. This scale is logarithmic, which means that each number is ten times stronger than the preceding number. For example, a pH of 2 is ten times more acidic than a pH of 3 and 100 times more acidic than a pH of 4.

The pH of your aquarium water is influenced by a variety of factors, including the amount of carbon dioxide and fish waste in the water. Goldfish hobbyists should maintain their pH somewhere between 6.5 and 8.5. This can be determined by using a pH test kit, which can be purchased at all aquarium supply shops. Commercial test kits that are very simple to use are available at most aquarium supply stores.

The pH level in your tank should be monitored every week or two to detect any changes. An abrupt drop in pH may be indicative of an increase in carbon dioxide or fish wastes. An increase in aeration or a partial water change may alleviate the problem.

Nitrogen

Nitrogenous wastes and ammonia are produced by the fish in your tank, and can build up to dangerous levels. Fortunately, they are naturally converted by the bacterial colonies in your tank into harmless products though a process called the nitrogen cycle (see the box below).

Since the nitrogen cycle occurs naturally, you might think that there's nothing to worry about when it comes to testing your water for nitrogen and its various compounds. Wrong! In new aquariums, many beginners experience "new tank syndrome," which occurs when the bacteria populations in your tank are not fully established, and so cannot cope with the waste buildup. Your fish suffer as a result.

This is generally not a problem for goldfish because they are so hardy, but it's not a bad idea to buy a nitrogen test kit for ammonia, nitrite, and nitrate when

The Nitrogen Cycle

Fish are living creatures that obtain energy from food and burn that energy with the help of oxygen they breathe from the water. These processes generate waste products that are returned to the environment via the gills and the digestive system. These wastes are primarily carbon dioxide and nitrogenous compounds such as ammonia.

In the aquarium, these wastes must be removed. Carbon dioxide generally leaves the water through aeration at the surface or through photosynthesis by aquarium plants. Toxic nitrogenous compounds are converted to less toxic compounds via the nitrogen cycle.

In nature, the nitrogen cycle (shown in the illustration on the next page) involves the conversion of toxic nitrogenous wastes and ammonia into harmless products by bacterial colonies. In short, bacteria drive the nitrogen cycle as they convert solid wastes and other organic debris (uneaten food) into ammonia, ammonia into nitrite, and nitrite into nitrate. Nitrate is then used by plants as fertilizer and is removed from the water. A healthy aquarium depends greatly on the nitrogen cycle to reduce toxic ammonia into less toxic nitrogen compounds.

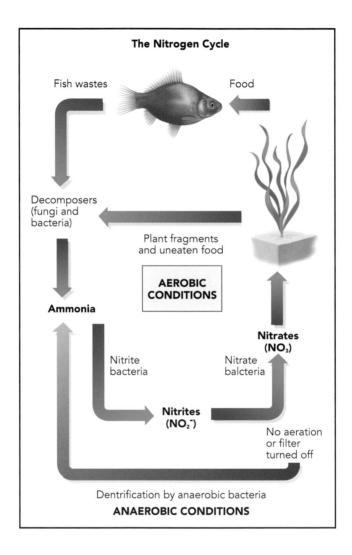

The Nitrogen Cycle

Fish wastes   Food

Decomposers
(fungi and
bacteria)

Plant fragments
and uneaten food

AEROBIC
CONDITIONS

Ammonia

Nitrates
(NO₃)

Nitrite
bacteria

Nitrate
balcteria

Nitrites
(NO₂⁻)

No aeration
or filter
turned off

Dentrification by anaerobic bacteria
ANAEROBIC CONDITIONS

starting up a new aquarium. Measure these compounds every week for the first couple of months after you start your aquarium. After this period, once a month is sufficient, unless you suspect a problem. You should see ammonia increase first, then decline as nitrite begins to elevate. As your bacteria colony flourishes, nitrite will decline as it is converted into nitrate, which increases slowly. Plants and frequent water changes will remove nitrate before it reaches toxic levels.

Don't take your fish out of the dark protective outer bag until you are ready to place it in the tank.

Bringing Your Goldfish Home

You will bring your goldfish home from the aquarium supply store in a clear plastic bag filled with water and oxygen. Ask to have this plastic bag placed into another bag—a paper bag or a dark opaque plastic bag, if possible. Try to resist the temptation to take the fish out in the light and gawk at it. Bringing the fish from the dark into the light and then back into dark will stress it. This weakens the fish and its resistance to other maladies. Keep it in the bag, in the dark, until you get home.

Placing the Fish in the Tank

It is important to follow the steps described here. While goldfish are hardy, they are not the best travelers, and may go into shock when they are transported and introduced into a new tank.

> **TIP**
>
> You really should buy and introduce all your goldfish within three to six weeks of one another. Introducing a new goldfish much later, after the existing fish have already set up certain territories and behavior patterns, may result in aggressive behavior, thereby disrupting the tank. All the fish should be of approximately the same size and age, as well.

1. When you get home, float the plastic bags of fish in the tank without opening them. This allows the temperature in the bag to acclimate to the temperature of the tank. Let the bags sit for at least ten to fifteen minutes.
2. Open the bag and let air in. Take a handful of water from the tank and pour it into the bag. Let the bag float this way for another ten minutes.
3. Now you can add the fish to the tank by opening the bag and gently inverting it into the tank, letting the fish out.

Chapter 5

Aquarium Plants

The one thing goldfish fanciers all know, though some won't admit it, is that goldfish are not especially kind to live plants. In most cases, goldfish treat plants the way we do potato chips—they munch on them. This is the best argument against live plants and for artificial ones.

Many experienced goldfish hobbyists know that to keep goldfish with live plants ultimately requires more care for the plants than for the fish themselves. You should consider how much time you want to devote to your aquarium before you decide between artificial and live plants. There are many goldfish experts who keep goldfish without any gravel or plants, but I don't find that aesthetically pleasing.

Another real advantage of artificial plants is that there are a lot of choices, and many of the better-made ones look like the real thing. As with most items you buy, the cheaper the artificial plants, the more plastic they look. Most of the better artificial plant manufacturers provide replicas of all the live plants described in this chapter.

Why Live Plants?

After what I've just said, why bother with live plants at all? First of all, as a result of photosynthesis, live plants are an excellent source of oxygen. They also absorb nitrates that build up in your fish tank. They provide shade, hiding places, egg-laying sites, and yes, even food for your goldfish.

Experienced goldfish enthusiasts keep two different kinds of plants in their aquariums: tough plants that cannot be easily eaten by goldfish, and smaller, more tender plants that are stocked to be eaten. The second group is provided so that the first group can grow successfully.

Plant Types

There are three major types of freshwater plants: rooted, bunches, and floaters. Rooted plants usually grow in numbers, but separate from one another. Bunches are plants that reproduce off one stem and can quickly envelop a tank. Floaters are floating plants whose root system dangles in the water. These usually grow near the surface, or in some cases right out of the water. Each of these groups have two or three varieties that can survive the onslaught of goldfish.

If you choose live plants, pick no more than two or three types—two is preferable. Pay attention to these plants and learn how to maintain them. The simpler you keep it, the faster and better you will learn to grow and keep plants. I would suggest arrowhead and pondweed. Both are hardy and difficult to kill. I recommend planting them to the back and sides of the tank, because if you are successful, your plants will grow large and you don't want them to obscure your view of the fish.

Don't give up if you kill the first set of plants—eventually you'll master this difficult phase of aquarium maintenance.

These plants are rooted in a jar that is set into the bottom gravel. This makes it almost impossible for the fish to uproot them.

Rooted Plants

There are three types of rooted plants that you should plant with goldfish: arrowhead, vallisneria, and Amazon sword plants. These do not appeal to goldfish as much as other plants might. But make no mistake: If they have mind to, goldfish will eventually destroy almost any plant.

Arrowhead and vallisneria are both stolon-type plants. That is, they reproduce by sending out a runner, which eventually grows into another plant. Wait until these new plants have developed a root system before separating them and planting them where you want.

These plants should be pruned whenever you see a brown patch on any part of them. Decay on most freshwater aquatic plants must be clipped off immediately, before it kills the plant and fouls the water.

Arrowhead

Arrowhead (*Sagittaria cuneata*) can grow up to 36 inches high. With long, straight leaves, they look best when placed in bunches. They are generally sturdy plants. For reproduction, you must cut runners from the stolon and replant them. Or you can weigh down the new plant with a thin lead band (available at your aquarium supply store) where you want it while it is still attached to the parent, and it will separate on its own. These plants can survive in temperatures as high as 77°F, but they are also hardy cold-water plants and do not require a lot of light to thrive.

Vallisneria

These are pretty, hardy plants. Vallisneria (*Vallisneria spiralis*) has long, ribbonlike leaves that spiral upward. It looks like a curly version of arrowhead and grows to about 2 feet long. For propagation, you must either cut the runner from the stolon and then plant it, or weigh down the new plant while it is still attached to the parent. These plants are not quite as hardy as arrowhead, as they have a more narrow temperature range of 59°F to 72°F.

Vallisneria has long, grasslike leaves.

The Amazon sword plant can survive above and below the water.

Amazon Sword Plant

The Amazon sword plant (*Echinodorus brevipedicellatus*) can have up to forty leaves, which are broad in the middle and tapered at each end. There is also a broad-leafed variety. This plant does well in medium to strong sunlight, or, alternatively, it should get about eight to ten hours of artificial light a day. It can survive in temperatures up to 80°F. Reproduction is similar to the previous two rooted types.

Bunched Plants

Given goldfish and their tendencies, I will mention only a few of the bunched plants that I believe are more than satisfactory in this type of environment. Pondweed and fox-tail offer the aquarist more than enough choice to make the aquascape interesting and healthy. These are plants that propagate by way of cuttings. Typically, you buy cuttings from your aquarium dealer. Slice off the bottom inch and take off many of the leaves along the next inch. Weigh down the bunch with a lead band and plant the bare inch of stem into the gravel. These plants take hold quickly and grow just as fast. Don't buy any plant that is already browning, as it will shortly be dead. Buy only completely green specimens.

Pondweed (Elodea)

Known as elodea or pondweed (*Anacharis canadensis*), this is a favorite for cold freshwater tanks. Pondweed is long, with narrow stalks that sprout rings of thick green leaves. In a regular tank, these plants need constant pruning, but this may or may not be the case in your goldfish tank. They grow so fast that they can even outgrow the hunger of a school of goldfish.

Pondweed is propagated by cutting off the lower inch when you buy it from your aquarium store and planting the remainder firmly in the gravel. The stems should be weighted. Generally speaking, this plant usually roots pretty quickly. They can withstand temperatures up to 80°F.

Foxtail (Milfoil)

Foxtail or milfoil (*Myriophyllum spicatum*) is another favorite in freshwater tanks. Given strong light, foxtail can sometimes grow 3 to 4 inches in a week's time. They look much like pondweed, except that they sprout much finer leaves, like eyelashes, in rings around the stalk. Otherwise, much of what is true for pondweed also holds true for foxtail.

Plants look best arranged in natural bunches. That's pondweed on the far right.

Floating Plants

Floating plants are highly recommended for goldfish but, unfortunately, for outdoor ponds only. These plants require large amounts of strong sunlight and generally grow much too large for the average aquarium. While they have been maintained by experts, they are not recommended for most aquarists. If your heart is set on floating plants, however, the three recommended are water hyacinth, duckweed, and crystalwort.

In strong light, foxtail (the tall, dark plant on the far right) can grow several inches in just a week.

Water hyacinth makes great shade for the fish and provides oxygen and nutrients.

Water Hyacinth

The water hyacinth (*Eichornia crassipes*) is a robust plant found all over the United States. It grows so quickly that it has been known to make waterways impassable. These plants provide great shade for the fish and make the water rich in both oxygen and nutrients. This is one of the best plants for goldfish, as the root system is also ideal for egg laying. When the flowers bloom, the plant may grow as tall as 12 inches. The flowers of water hyacinths that are grown indoors last for less than twenty-four hours.

Duckweed can quickly cover a small pond. You may find your goldfish pond attracts a lot of visitors, including frogs.

Duckweed

Duckweed (*Lemna minor*) floats on top of the water in no fewer than two egg-shaped leaves at a time. They have a single root. These are much more delicate plants than water hyacinths, but are still pretty hardy. They propagate quickly. Like water hyacinths and water lilies, duckweed can quickly cover a small pond. It needs lots of light.

Crystalwort

Crystalwort (*Riccia fluitans*) is an ideal plant for goldfish. It can be used for egg laying, for nourishment, and for shade. Its root system is softer than the hyacinth's and allows for various uses by adult goldfish, as well as their small fry. It needs a minimum of six hours of light a day. The only danger is that they do tend to have parasites. When you buy them, make sure you choose only the healthiest-looking specimens.

Chapter 6

The Outdoor Goldfish Pond

Goldfish are excellent garden pond and pool fish. They were originally bred from wild carp and are therefore coldwater, freshwater fish. Along with their cousins the Koi, goldfish are among the hardiest and most easily kept pond fish.

There are similarities and differences between keeping an aquarium and keeping a pond. For example, there is generally no heater in a pond. And making a pond is more complicated than simply going out into your backyard and digging a hole for your goldfish.

Where to Place the Pond

This is a tricky question, because goldfish need plenty of sunlight and plenty of shade. The sunlight keeps the water relatively warm, which keeps the goldfish healthy and active. But if too much of the pond is in the sun, it will be overrun by algae. Therefore, the pond should always be partially shaded. Goldfish will use that part of the pond to cool off when the sunny side gets too warm.

Goldfish will also use these shaded areas to hide from the prying eyes of predators. Aquarium enthusiasts don't need to worry about predators, but pond-keepers do. Depending on where you live, there are a number of wild animals that would love a nice fish dinner, including all kinds of birds (including ducks, swans, geese, and osprey), a few snakes, raccoons, weasels, skunks, turtles, and many house pets. For protection, it is always a good idea to keep a lot of water hyacinths or duckweed for the fish to hide under. A fence around the pond will also keep out some of these hungry predators.

> ## Is Your Climate Right?
>
> This is a question you really should ask your local aquarium dealer. If you live in a temperate zone, you should be able to keep a pond. But if it gets too cold in your area during the winter and your pond will likely freeze solid, it will kill the fish. In that case, you should be prepared to winter your goldfish indoors. And that can mean some *very* big tanks!

Pond Size

Just like your fish tank, your pond should be wide and long, to give your fish as much surface area as possible. The pond should be no more than 3 to 4 feet deep. Remember, you need access to your fish, so don't make the pond too deep or it will be impossible to catch them. The pond should also be large enough so that sudden outside temperature changes won't affect the temperature of the water too quickly.

If you are considering breeding goldfish in the pond, make sure to leave a shallow area approximately 12 inches deep for spawning. The fish will naturally spawn there, so be sure to have plenty of plant life. This is also a good place to feed your fish, so that you can see them clearly and enjoy them more fully.

The rule for ponds is 30 square inches of water per 1 inch of fish. In general, the larger the space, the faster your goldfish will grow. Within a year to a year and a half, a 6-month-old goldfish with a lot of room will grow to be almost 18 inches long.

Types of Ponds

Pools and ponds can be made of many different things, including old large bathtubs, children's large one-piece plastic pools, or strong wood frames with layers of heavy-duty plastic sheeting. They can be many different shapes and sizes.

There are basically three kinds of ponds. First, there is the molded pond, which is usually a solid one-piece unit. The molded pool is placed into a pit, which should be lined with about 6 inches of sand. This way, as the unit settles

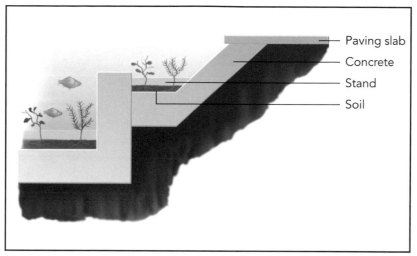

— Paving slab
— Concrete
— Stand
— Soil

A concrete pond must be thick and nonporous.

under the weight of the water, the pond can be leveled slightly before it is completely filled.

The lined pond has one or more heavy-duty plastic sheets lining a deep hole. The hole should be at least 3 to 4 feet deep at the deepest point, but should slope gently on all sides. Make sure the bottom of the hole is smooth, with no rocks or roots to pierce the lining. Again, spreading a layer of sand is a good way to smooth out the bottom. The plastic sheet liner should overhang the hole 12 to 18 inches on all sides. Water can then be poured in. After the sheet has taken on the shape of the pond, place large rocks or slate slabs on the edges to keep the sheet from moving. The rocks also serve to hide the plastic material.

Finally, some folks prefer a concrete pond. If you are ambitious enough to build a concrete pond, make sure the walls and bottom are thick and that the concrete is not porous. The bottom should be up to 12 inches thick and the walls at least 4 inches thick. The shape of the pond is up to you.

Of course, you can have a much more ambitious pond built by a contractor who specializes in such things. Ask your local aquarium dealer or landscaper, if you are so inclined.

> ### T I P
> Waterfalls provide activity and beauty. If you have one, the mist forms an excellent environment where plants will thrive. The falling water mixes with air, providing excellent aeration, and keeps the pond water from stagnating.

Filtration

It is best, of course, to provide filtration for your pond. There are many kinds of pond filters. Consult with your aquarium dealer and choose a filter that is right for the size of your pond. Pond filters are larger and more industrial-looking than those used by the indoor hobbyist. These filters are also more expensive.

Goldfish can live in unfiltered ponds, but there must be a lot of surface area for sufficient air exchange. As long as the number of fish is not too great, your pond should be fine. If it is feasible and not too expensive, placing an aerator in an unfiltered pond is an excellent idea. It will keep the water moving and oxygenate it.

The Fish

As noted in chapter 3, there are several varieties of goldfish that can live well in a pond. Here are some of the hardier of the pond breeds. Any of these, with metallic or calico coloration, will be fine.

- Common Goldfish
- Comet

Very large goldfish can coexist with Koi like this one in an outdoor pond.

- Black Moor
- Fantail
- Pearl-Scale
- Shubunkin
- Wakins

Depending on where you live, the Bubble-Eye and the Black Bubble-Eye are also considered hardy enough for pond life. The weather must be relatively warm and there should be no sharp edges anywhere in the pond. As is the case with an indoor aquarium, you should keep only similar fish together. Chapters 3 and 4 give you some guidance about what types of goldfish can live together. Take size into account as well, because ponds support larger fish. A 12-inch goldfish will not tolerate a 2-inch goldfish for very long—especially if the bigger fish is hungry.

Pond Plants

For the outdoor goldfish enthusiast, ideal plants include water hyacinth, duckweed, crystalwort, and water lily. However, water lilies don't thrive in moving water. Instead, they should be packed in a bucket with firm but not hard-packed dirt, topped with large gravel. Fill the bucket with water after the lilies have been planted and place it at the center of the pond. Water lilies are very hardy and can be left out all year as long as there is water in the pond, even if it freezes. Just make sure there are no fish in the pond if it freezes.

If you want to plant pondweed, vallisneria, or any other anchored plant, you need to put a few inches of soil on the pond floor. On top of that, you should probably put another couple of inches of sand or large gravel. Make sure to rinse the sand or gravel thoroughly before placing it in the pond. However, don't use large gravel if you are going to stock the pond with Bubble-Eye goldfish, because it can injure them.

Feeding

There's good news and there's bad news. The bad news is that you have just supplied the local insects with the best place in the world to breed—a more or less stagnant pond near a house full of humans. Mosquitoes are going to love that! The good news is that your goldfish will love it even more. Those mosquitoes and their larvae will never make it out alive. Many local insects will use your

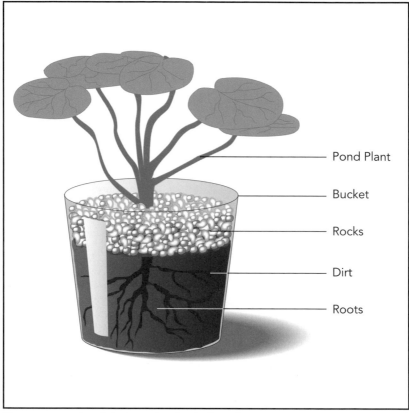

You can put your plants in buckets and set them in the pond.

pond for breeding. But don't worry; if they do, your fish will be supplied with an excellent food source and a tasty treat supplied by Mother Nature herself.

The feeding instructions remain the same as for fish kept indoors (see chapter 7), only more so. In the late summer and autumn, feed your pond fish three times a day with high-carbohydrate foods. This is important for pond fish because they do not eat much during the winter months—nor should they.

In the winter, goldfish settle in the mud and do very little. The cold temperatures reduce their metabolic rate and keep them from being active. You should feed them once a day and only enough for them to eat in five minutes. Don't overfeed them in the winter or the spring.

Spawning and Breeding

Spawning occurs very naturally for pond fish, especially those kept outside year round. They winter naturally and come into spring ready to spawn.

The partial shading in your pond prevents the growth of too much algae, and algae prevent goldfish from spawning. However, make sure to have some crystalwort in the pond for the fish to lay their eggs on.

If you plan to raise the fry in the pond, remember to take out the adult fish, or else the fry will be eaten. It may be easier, however, to remove the fry and raise them elsewhere.

Cleaning the Pond

While vacuuming is critical to maintaining the health of an indoor aquarium, skimming is best for an outdoor pond. Any type of skimmer can be used, so you are better off buying one at a pool equipment store than at an aquarium store, where you're likely to find a better selection. Use the skimmer to take large debris out of the pond and keep the water surface clear.

Algae can also be an enemy of the outdoor fish hobbyist. Although algae oxygenate the water, too much can eventually foul it. You need to keep an eye on the algae situation at all times. Heavy algal growth that clouds the water should be removed with the skimmer.

The pond needs to be pumped out annually so that you can clean it properly. Follow the instructions for cleaning in chapter 8. Ammonia and other nitrogenous compounds can build up in your pond. So every couple of months you should attempt a water change of some size—perhaps 30 to 75 gallons if you have a large pond, and 10 or 20 gallons if you have a small one.

Use the skimmer to remove debris and algae from your pond.

Part III

Taking Care of Your Goldfish

Chapter 7

Feeding Your Goldfish

Goldfish can survive a lifetime on flake foods. However, if you want active, colorful, healthy fish, you must vary their diets. If you have any interest in breeding your goldfish, plan on investing some time and energy into establishing a healthier feeding regimen. While flake food is a pretty good source of nutrition, use it as a staple and substitute other foods a few times every week to ensure your fish get a balanced diet.

The foods you provide for your goldfish should supply them with the same essential nutrients that all animals need. Proteins, vitamins, and minerals are obviously important for growth and sustenance, but they are particularly important for exotic goldfish with any kind of head growth, such as Lionheads, Orandas, and Pompons. Fats and carbohydrates are, of course, necessary for energy. Fat storage is important for fish that live outdoors so they can sustain themselves through the winter months. Fiber provides the diet with bulk and is important for a healthy digestive system. So the bottom line is that goldfish should regularly eat something from the vegetable, cereal, and fish or meat food groups.

What Should I Feed My Goldfish?

There are as many different types of food for your goldfish as there are different types of goldfish. However, all these foods can be grouped into four basic food categories: prepared flake foods, frozen or freeze-dried foods, live foods, and household foods. There is, of course, flake food, which generally provides your

A varied, healthy diet will help your goldfish maintain their beautiful colors.

goldfish with a very balanced diet. This prepared food contains the essential nutrients for a long and happy life. However, there are other types of food you can provide to vary the diet.

Frozen or freeze-dried foods are really the hobbyist's best friend. They are an excellent source of protein and goldfish love them. More important, they offer all the benefits of live foods without the risks.

Live foods are risky because, with the exception of earthworms and brine shrimp, many of them can carry harmful pathogens that may infect or even kill your fish. On the other hand, they are the most natural way for your fish to eat. Goldfish will eat all kinds of worms: red worms, white worms, earthworms, and tubifex. They will also eat brine shrimp, mosquito larvae, and fruit flies.

Household foods are also an excellent source of nutrition. Goldfish love almost any kind of seafood—crab, lobster, oysters, clams—either fresh or canned. In the vegetable world, they can be fed canned vegetables, such as beans, which are especially good for them, or fresh veggies, such as spinach, broccoli, and cauliflower.

> Goldfish are considered omnivores because they eat everything—as opposed to carnivores, which only eat meat, and herbivores, which only eat vegetables.

Flake Foods

Flake and dried foods are available in a wide variety of shapes and sizes from many, many manufacturers. The most important thing to know is that goldfish do not have the same nutritional needs as tropical fish. Their body makeup and composition are substantially different. Consequently, fish food manufacturers produce flake and dried foods especially for goldfish that meet their unique nutritional requirements. Make sure you choose one of these. Many dried food manufacturers are also marketing feeding kits that promise to improve growth and color. Don't buy these kits unless they are developed exclusively for goldfish.

Dried foods can be produced in a number of ways, including flakes and pellets, also known as granules (which are bite-size chunks) or tablets (the largest of the consumable compressed dried foods). Some manufacturers make vitamin-enriched flake food, but supplementing isn't necessary if you follow the feeding guidelines in this book.

Frozen or Freeze-dried Foods

Frozen or freeze-dried foods offer the best of the live world without any of the hassles of keeping it alive. They are also disease free. These foods include brine shrimp, krill (shrimp a little larger than brine), tubifex worms, mosquito larvae, daphnia, and bloodworms. This type of food is convenient if you want to provide variety for your fish without too much fuss.

Freeze-dried brine shrimp are convenient and nutritious.

Live Foods

Live foods are easily the best food to give your always-hungry goldfish, but, as we've already mentioned, these foods carry the risk of introducing harmful pathogens into both your goldfish and your aquarium.

Although many experts actually cultivate their own live food, I strongly recommend against it for beginners. Live foods can easily be obtained in small quantities from your local aquarium supply store and can usually be bought in one- or two-serving sizes. The live food you get at your local store is also pretty safe, since the store owner is probably feeding it to their own fish.

The only two live foods that generally do not have the potential to carry disease are earthworms and brine shrimp. Both are readily available and are excellent additions to your fish's diet.

> ### CAUTION
>
> No matter what you've been told, it is not a good idea to go searching in lakes or ponds for live foods. Since most of these are larvae, they tend to be in murky, stagnant water, where they are most likely to pick up parasites and other infectious agents.

Brine Shrimp

The brine shrimp (*Artemia* species) is a primitive crustacean that inhabits salt ponds in more than 160 locations around the world. Those in your local aquarium supply store probably originated in San Francisco Bay or Great Salt Lake in Utah. They are one of the best sources of nutrition available for aquarium organisms of any type. Brine shrimp are an excellent source of fat and protein. Of all the live food available, they are the safest because they do not carry disease. Besides, goldfish love them!

An added advantage to brine shrimp is that you can raise them yourself; many dealers sell brine shrimp eggs. To raise brine shrimp, it is best to follow the instructions accompanying the eggs.

Earthworms

Earthworms are rich in protein and offer some variety to your goldfish's diet. They are particularly valuable to hobbyists and enjoyed by goldfish during or just before breeding season. And they are easily obtained. You can search for them after rain showers on lawns and around ponds, as long as you make sure no herbicides or weed killers have been used in the area where you are collecting your worms. Pesticides will poison your fish.

You can also cultivate them in your backyard. In my opinion, this is the only live food that a beginner should cultivate. Earthworms can be cultivated by setting aside a small patch of dirt, maybe a yard or two square, and throwing a couple of burlap sacks over the raw, tilled soil. Then, with a garden hose, wet the burlap sacks until they are saturated. Do this every morning for a week. On the seventh day, lift up the burlap sacks, and bingo, worm city! I don't recommend that you take too many to feed your fish right away, nor do I recommend that you harvest them more than once a week. The best time to harvest is usually early in the morning, before the dew has evaporated.

Your fish will enjoy hunting and eating live foods. But they do carry risks.

Before feeding earthworms to your goldfish, rinse them and put them in a jar with holes in the lid; let them sit for a day or two in a dark, shaded area. Rinse them each day as they rid their bodies of any earth they have inside of them. Then cut them into small bits so your fish can eat them. If you have small goldfish (less than 4 inches long), you really should dice them up. If your goldfish are larger (4 to 6 inches long), cut the worms into halves or thirds. Any goldfish over 6 inches long will be more than happy to swallow whole worms.

Tubifex Worms

Also known as sludgeworms, these long, thin, red worms are not very pretty, but are readily available at your local aquarium supply store, where their chance of carrying disease is low. Like all live food, they are an excellent source of nutrition and will be appreciated by your fish.

Whiteworms

Also known as microworms, these worms are white or beige. They can be bought in single-serving amounts from your local aquarium supply store.

Daphnia

Also known as water flea larvae, these are an excellent food for your goldfish. However, goldfish should be fed daphnia in moderation, since too much can act as a laxative and cause serious digestive problems. Moderation is the key to everything. Daphnia are easily obtained in small quantities from your local aquarium supply store.

Drosophila

These are the larvae of the wingless (actually, vestigial-winged) fruit fly, so they won't try to fly around your house. They provide your fish with a tasty treat and an excellent food source. You can sometimes buy them at the local aquarium supply store.

Bloodworms

Also known as two-winged fly larvae, bloodworms are usually in good supply year round and can be purchased at your local aquarium supply store. Because they are difficult to culture, they are commercially bred and therefore offer less risk to the hobbyist. Again, these can be bought in small quantities for single or double servings.

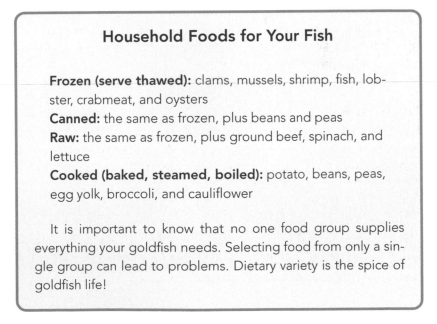

Household Foods for Your Fish

Frozen (serve thawed): clams, mussels, shrimp, fish, lobster, crabmeat, and oysters
Canned: the same as frozen, plus beans and peas
Raw: the same as frozen, plus ground beef, spinach, and lettuce
Cooked (baked, steamed, boiled): potato, beans, peas, egg yolk, broccoli, and cauliflower

It is important to know that no one food group supplies everything your goldfish needs. Selecting food from only a single group can lead to problems. Dietary variety is the spice of goldfish life!

Household Foods

Household foods offer nutritional value and great variety to the goldfish diet. You can offer your goldfish fresh, frozen, or canned oysters, clams, mussels, crabmeat, lobster, or bits of raw fish—but no canned tuna fish if it is packed in oil. Baked or boiled beans, steamed cauliflower or broccoli, and boiled or baked potato are all excellent additions as well. Fresh lettuce or spinach is also good. Raw bits of ground beef are especially prized.

Household foods have to be given in moderation and must be diced or shredded for your fish. Don't offer your fish just any table scraps—only high-quality food will do. And make sure the food has no spices—not even salt.

How to Feed Your Fish

The biggest problem when feeding goldfish is that they will eat to the point of bursting. They are gluttons—and that's the nicest thing that can be said about their eating habits. Their food intake must be controlled. It is best to feed goldfish about as much as they can eat in five minutes. Do this twice a day, morning and night, and always in the same part of the tank.

Only feed your fish as much as they can eat in five minutes.

A Sample Diet

The following is a sample diet for thirty days. This is simply a suggestion, to give you an idea of how to vary your goldfish's diet. You can make substitutions, of course, but you must make sure to balance one group with another.

You need not attempt to feed every different kind of food to your goldfish. If you buy any kind of worms or cultivate anything on your own, for that month or two your fish will have a steady diet of that particular kind of food. In the diet listed below, I assumed that you have cultivated your own brine shrimp and earthworms. Along with dried food as the staple, I mixed in a few vegetables and some other proteins.

Day 1	Dried food	Day 16	Earthworms
Day 2	Earthworms	Day 17	Dried food
Day 3	Dried food	Day 18	Brine shrimp
Day 4	Brine shrimp	Day 19	Dried food
Day 5	Dried food	Day 20	Raw, torn spinach
Day 6	Raw, torn spinach	Day 21	Dried food
Day 7	Dried food	Day 22	Canned clams
Day 8	Cooked egg yolks	Day 23	Earthworms
Day 9	Earthworms	Day 24	Dried food
Day 10	Dried food	Day 25	Baked beans
Day 11	Brine shrimp	Day 26	Dried food
Day 12	Dried food	Day 27	Canned clams
Day 13	Baked beans	Day 28	Dried food
Day 14	Dried food	Day 29	Raw ground beef
Day 15	Dried food	Day 30	Earthworm

To begin, put some flake food on the water and let them eat. If they finish all or most of it before the five minutes are up, add a little more. Use the same method with live, freeze-dried, or household food. It's that easy.

If you go away for a weekend, don't worry about feeding the fish. They can go up to three weeks without being fed—although they certainly won't be happy about it!

When feeding your fish, remember that it's always better to underfeed than to overfeed. Overfeeding can cause health and water-quality problems, while feeding a bit too little won't hurt anything.

Rules for Feeding Goldfish

- Only feed them what they can eat in five minutes.
- Feed them at the same time every day, once in the morning, once at night.
- Always feed them at the same spot in the tank.
- Don't overfeed the fish, no matter how humane you think you are being. More goldfish die, especially older ones, from overeating than from anything else.

Chapter 8

Maintaining Your Aquarium

Y ou have two really important things that you need to do every day. First, turn the aquarium light on in the morning and off in the evening. Light is important for both the fish and the plants (if you have live ones). And, as we have already learned, fish need their sleep. Second, remember to feed your fish every day. You need to do this at the same place in the tank each time and around the same time each morning and night.

Otherwise, the most important thing that any fish hobbyist can do is pay attention. Get to know your fish, watch how they interact, and make note of any unusual behavior. You should closely watch your fish for signs of disease and look at the way they interact to see if any are being picked on. Check the plants to see if any parts of them are dying. If they are, remove the brown sections at once.

The more stable you make the conditions in your aquarium, the less likely you are to stress your fish. Rapid or frequent fluctuations in water temperature and water quality cause stress and therefore compromise the health of your fish. You must monitor the water temperature, making sure it remains constant. Examine the filter, the heater, and the airstones to make sure they are in good working order. The filter may have a blockage, especially if you are using a box filter. The thermostat light in the heater should be working properly. Make sure the air pump and airstones are operating at maximum efficiency. These things should be checked daily or weekly, and require just a few moments of your time. While you are feeding or simply enjoying your pets, you can perform a routine check of the tank components and the aquarium occupants.

General Maintenance

Keeping the fish tank clean involves a real commitment, and is not for the lazy. You must have a regular maintenance schedule, and you must take care at every step. Your goldfish's lives depend on your attention to detail, because healthy fish can only live in a healthy tank.

Vacuum the Bottom

Weekly vacuuming is one of the most important aspects of maintaining your tank. Eventually, fish wastes, plant fragments, and uneaten food accumulate at the bottom of your tank. You must prevent the buildup of this waste and debris in the gravel. It is very important to remove this detritus, because it breaks down into ammonia and other compounds, which are not good for your fish.

Vacuuming is important even if you have an undergravel filter, because you don't want the waste building up in the gravel and impeding the flow of water through the filter.

Vacuum weekly to keep waste from building up in your tank.

Check the Filter

Remember to check the filter media once a week. The top-level filter floss gets dirty quickly and easily, as this is the stage that collects the most debris. If there is a buildup of waste in your box or power filter, it will reduce the flow of water through the filter and reduce the filter's efficiency.

Every month, rinse the filter media under lukewarm water until the water is clear. You should probably replace about 50 percent of the media every month, making sure to reuse about half of the old filter material. This way, the beneficial bacterial colony in your filter media will not be thrown out and you won't have to start from scratch. One of the most common mistakes that new aquarists make is replacing all the filter media because it looks dirty. But some of that "dirt" includes bacteria that are beneficial to the filtering process.

Activated carbon becomes ineffective after a month or two, so that should all be dumped and replaced. For filters that use cartridges as filter media, check with the manufacturer for optimum maintenance and replacement frequency.

Scrape the Algae

Algae is the soft brown-green plantlike moss that develops all over your tank and everything in it. It develops faster in some tanks than in others, depending on the proximity to sunlight and the amount of nitrates in the water, which fertilize the algae.

At lower levels, algae perform the same beneficial tasks that all plants do. However, algae can overrun your tank, cloud your water, and ultimately choke your tank. It is important to stop too much algal growth by simply scraping off the algae. Algae scrapers are either sponges attached to a long stick or a pair of magnetized scrapers that enable you to clean the inside of the aquarium walls from the outside. If you have too much algae that refuses to go away, it's a good indication that you need to get rid of excess nitrates— and that means a partial water change.

> ### CAUTION
>
> Never use soap to clean anything in your tank. It always leaves a residue, no matter how much you rinse. Plain water and elbow grease are always the best weapons against dirt and algae.

Test the Water

When you first set up the aquarium, testing the water every couple of days is critical to the water maturation process. As you begin to add fish, water chemistry changes radically and water-quality monitoring is critical to the survival of your fish. After this sensitive period of two to four weeks, it is still very

Make sure the water your fish are living in is healthy and clean.

important to test your water, and I recommend that you do so every two weeks for the first two months, as described in chapter 4. This gives you a good understanding of the mechanics of the nitrogen cycle. Water testing also tells you when the nitrates have risen to the point where a water change is needed.

After two months, your tank will be well established and the need to test the water every week diminishes. At this point, a monthly water test will suffice unless you suspect you might have tank problems. Sudden behavioral changes in your fish, fish disease, fish mortality, excessive algal growth, smelly water, and cloudy water all warrant an immediate water-quality test and a possible water change.

Partial Water Changes

Partial water changes are one of the most important aspects of maintaining your aquarium. A partial water change is when you take out a quarter, a third, or half of the existing water in the tank and replace it with new water. The amount you change is up to you, depending on the water quality of your tank. But remember, goldfish are messy and water quality is important. Partial water changes go a long way toward maintaining good water quality.

Partial water changes help maintain good water quality because each time you change the water, you are diluting the amount of nitrogenous compounds such as nitrites and nitrates, harmful gases, and other toxic substances. The water you add is more oxygen rich than the water in your tank.

The best time to do a partial water change is while you are vacuuming your tank. Otherwise, you can use a siphon and a large bucket. The siphon is basically just a 3- or 4-foot hose or tube that will transfer water from the tank to the bucket.

How to Siphon Water

1. Fill the siphon tube completely with water, making sure there is no trapped air anywhere in the tube. Make sure the siphon is clean and your hands are clean as well. You can fill the hose at the sink or by submerging it in the aquarium. Only do the latter if your aquarium is large enough to accommodate the tube without spooking the fish. Use your thumbs to block both ends of the siphon to keep the water in and the air out.

2. Keeping your thumbs in place, place one end of the tube in the aquarium and aim the other at the bucket. Make sure the bucket end is lower than the aquarium or siphoning will not work. If you filled your siphon in the aquarium, plug one end of the tube tightly, lift it from the aquarium and lower it to the bucket.

3. Release your thumbs and the water will begin to flow rapidly from the aquarium into the bucket.

Fill the siphon tube with water and use your thumbs to block both ends.

Put one end of the tube in the aquarium and the other end in the bucket. Release your thumbs and water will flow from the tank.

Maintenance Checklist

Daily

- [ ] Feed the goldfish twice a day.
- [ ] Turn the tank lights on and off.
- [ ] Check the water temperature.
- [ ] Make sure the filter is in working order.
- [ ] Make sure the aerator is working.

Weekly

- [ ] Study the fish for signs of disease.
- [ ] Add water to make up for any evaporated water.
- [ ] Check the filter to see if the top mat needs to be replaced.
- [ ] Vacuum the tank thoroughly to clean up waste.
- [ ] Test the water for pH, nitrates, and hardness (first two months).
- [ ] Trim any brown portions of live plants.

Monthly

- [ ] Change 25 percent of the water.
- [ ] Clean the tank's glass on the inside using an algae scraper.
- [ ] Vacuum the tank thoroughly, stirring up the gravel.
- [ ] Rinse the filter media completely; replace half.
- [ ] Replace activated carbon.
- [ ] Wash off any tank decorations that have dirt or algae buildup.

Yearly

- [ ] Replace the airstones.
- [ ] Thoroughly wash all the gravel.
- [ ] Clean the inside of the tank thoroughly.

Some hobbyists use the siphon to vacuum the bottom of the tank. This kills two birds with one stone, so to speak. But you must make sure your hose is of sufficient diameter to siphon up the larger pieces of debris. No matter what tools you use, you must do both—vacuum the gravel and make partial water changes.

Do not add water straight from the faucet to your tank. Age the water at least twenty-four to forty-eight hours by keeping it in a bunch of one-gallon jugs stored in the house.

Chapter 9

Goldfish Diseases

Goldfish are subject to all kinds of diseases. Many are introduced with new fish, and some are highly contagious. Whether disease breaks out depends on the resistance of your fish. Poor living conditions weaken your fish, cause chronic stress, and ultimately compromise the fish's immune system. This is why I have repeatedly stressed the importance of maintaining a healthy aquarium for your pets. Even if you do everything in your power to maintain a disease-free aquarium, you may have to confront health problems in your fish; even experts fall victim to these problems.

Remember, healthy goldfish rarely get sick. When they do, it usually means that they have been stressed by poor water conditions, rapid temperature changes, bad lighting, bad food, or any number of other factors associated with an unhealthy aquarium. It is important to maintain your aquarium carefully so that you don't have to read this chapter again.

Signs of Illness

The first step in treating any kind of ailment in your aquarium is to recognize and identify the problem. You can determine if a fish is not healthy by its appearance and its behavior. Since you have been spending time examining your fish while you feed them, you should be able to identify problems as soon as they manifest themselves.

Telltale behavioral signs of illness include:

- Lack of appetite
- Hyperventilation of the gills (the fish looks like it is panting)
- Gasping for air near the surface
- Erratic swimming behavior
- Lack of movement
- Rubbing the body or fins against objects in the tank
- Twitching fins

External symptoms include a variety of physical abnormalities of the head, body, fins, gills, scales, and anal vent. The key to diagnosing the various diseases associated with aquarium fish is to learn the signs of each one.

Commercial Remedies

When you are a beginner, it is very important to use commercially available treatments rather than homemade remedies. Some experts recommend using chemicals such as malachite green or potassium permanganate to treat fish diseases. These chemicals must be handled in very exact doses. If a fish is overdosed with one of them, it can kill the fish faster than the disease. Especially with fancy goldfish, you must be cautious.

Discuss all the possible remedies for a disease with your local aquarium supply dealer. If you are still not satisfied, don't be afraid to call your veterinarian and ask a few questions. If your veterinarian does not treat fish, he or she can usually recommend someone who does. Finally, when you apply the remedy, make sure you follow the directions *exactly*.

The Old-Fashioned Salt Bath

This is the most time-tested cure-all of the freshwater fish world. Sometimes called the progressive saltwater treatment, it is how the hospital tank (see the box on page 104) is most often used. This very simple treatment has been known to cure a number of fish diseases, including ich, fungus, velvet, and tail rot. Many experts swear by it.

You simply add one teaspoon of table salt (not iodized) for each gallon of water to the hospital tank that houses your sick fish. Add the same amount of salt again that night and twice the next day, also in the morning and at night. If there is no improvement by the third or fourth day, add one more teaspoon of

Any difficulty swimming is a sign of illness.

salt each day. On the ninth and tenth days, make partial water changes and check for results.

Emergency Cleaning

If any of the infestations mentioned in this chapter strike more than three or four fish, you need to take drastic measures and perform an emergency cleaning. This is the most extreme treatment for disease in your aquarium. Place all the fish in the hospital tank and begin treating them. Then turn your attention to the aquarium.

An emergency cleaning means breaking down and thoroughly cleaning your aquarium and starting it up again from scratch. Throw out filter media and empty out the contents of the tank. Wash the walls, the gravel, and the filter with bleach. Of course, make sure you rinse everything thoroughly. Then rinse it all again. Do the same with the plastic plants.

Throw out the rocks and buy new ones. If you have any live plants, dispose of them too. Replace the filter media and airstones, any tubing, and whatever else you have in the tank. Wash the heater with bleach as well, making sure to rinse it thoroughly. In essence, you are starting over again because your tank was overrun by disease.

The Hospital Tank

One of the best ways to treat any fish is to separate it from the rest of the group as quickly as possible in a separate tank known as a hospital tank. There are a lot of reasons to have a hospital tank. First, many fish maladies are contagious. Any time you think you might have a diseased fish, it's always best to isolate it at least until you can determine whether the problem is contagious. Also, diseased or weak fish will often get picked on by healthier fish. Goldfish are no exception, and their bedside manner can be less than sympathetic. Also, it's obviously easier to observe the fish when it's by itself.

Some of the problems listed below require treatment, which is sometimes as simple as a change of diet. However, when feeding your goldfish medicated food, it is important to make sure that the right fish gets the medication. You don't want to medicate a healthy fish. This is another good reason to isolate sick fish.

The hospital tank need not be large; a 10-gallon tank will do if your goldfish are not very large. It does need adequate filtration and aeration, but plants and gravel should be left out. Try to provide some kind of cover for the fish in the form of rocks or empty flowerpots as a source of security.

Common Diseases

There are hundreds of maladies that can afflict goldfish. Not all are common in the average home aquarium. The following provides a general overview of the diseases you are most likely to encounter in your aquarium. For a more complete listing of goldfish diseases and their treatments, consult the references in the appendix.

Constipation or Indigestion (not contagious)

A fish that is constipated or suffering from indigestion is often very inactive and usually rests on the bottom of the tank. Its abdomen generally swells or bulges. This can be caused by an incorrect diet, food that doesn't agree with the fish, or overfeeding. You will need to change the food you are feeding this fish.

Isolate the fish in a hospital tank (see the box above). Don't feed the fish for three to five days, until it returns to being active. When it resumes normal behavior, feed it live or freeze-dried food for one week. After one week, return the fish to its normal tank. This is a problem that tends to recur, so make it a point to watch this fish.

This is especially a problem with Tosakins, Ryunkins, Veiltails, and Pearl-Scales.

Dropsy or Kidney Bloat (may be contagious)

This is also known as aeromonas, or pinecone disease because the fish's belly bloats noticeably and the scales stick out like a pinecone. In general, this disease causes the body to swell due to a buildup of fluid in the tissues. It is thought to be caused by water-quality problems or some kind of organ failure.

Many of the exotic goldfish varieties are slow and less active than typical aquarium fish. Know what is normal for your fish and you will be able to notice subtle changes that may indicate a problem.

Fish generally don't live more than a week after the signs of full-blown dropsy are manifested, although some fish have survived. Like constipation and swim bladder disease, fish that survive dropsy tend to have recurring attacks. While dropsy is not thought to be contagious, it is best to remove the fish at once. The tank should have an emergency cleaning.

Many experts believe dropsy is untreatable and that the fish should be immediately removed and painlessly destroyed. Others believe medicated food is one way to treat dropsy. Still others suggest mixing Furanance (an antibiotic) with water, 250 milligrams to the gallon. This bath should last only an hour and should not be repeated more than three times in three days. It is thought that goldfish can absorb Furanance through the skin. If you decide not to use Furanance, try the old-fashioned salt bath (see page 102).

> ### CAUTION
>
> Constipation and swim bladder problems must be taken seriously and treated quickly—they are among the leading causes of death in goldfish.

Pop-Eye (not contagious)

This disease, also known as exophthalmus, causes the eyes to bulge from their sockets in a very abnormal way. It can be difficult to diagnose because sometimes people think that they bought the wrong variety of goldfish. There is no cure. It usually happens to Common Goldfish, Comets, Shubunkins, and the like. As long as the fish does not seem to suffer and goes on living a normal life, there is no reason to act.

Swim Bladder Disease (not contagious)

This is a fairly easy disease to diagnose, because an infected fish can't swim properly. This happens mostly to the egg-shaped goldfish, both with and without dorsal fins. A goldfish with swim bladder disease swims on its side or upside-down, or even somersaults as it attempts to swim. Swim bladder disease can result from constipation, from bruising of the swim bladder during handling, fighting, or breeding, or from bacterial infection associated with poor water quality. This disease is sometimes caused by changes in temperature that most often occur when a fish is transported.

Detected and diagnosed early, it is treatable with isolation and medicated food. Detected too late, the results are irreversible—it is a deadly disease.

Sometimes a sick fish can be found at the bottom or at the top of the tank. If it's a female, she might be carrying eggs. If not, try the old-fashioned salt bath (see page 102).

Poor water quality will make your fish vulnerable to disease. A healthy tank houses healthy fish.

Swim bladder problems sometimes right themselves. But, like constipation or indigestion, once your fish has developed this painful problem, it is more likely to have a recurrence. Wait for the fish to right itself. You might want to feed your fish some medicated food; your aquarium supply store owner will be able to direct you. And, in general, feed your fish something else, because diet is one of the biggest reasons this problem develops.

If you suspect a bacterial infection, improve water quality and treat the fish with a broad-spectrum antibiotic.

Tumors (usually not contagious)

Obvious lumps, bumps, or protrusions, tumors sometimes look like large blisters or warts. They have been known to grow to the size of large screw heads. They can be surgically removed but only by a veterinarian.

Bacterial, Viral, and Fungal Infections

Body Slime Fungus (highly contagious)

This deadly affliction can kill your fish in two days if not caught in time. The protective mucous coating grows white and starts peeling off as if the fish were shedding its skin. The fins are gradually covered as well. Eventually, the body becomes red with irritation.

Call your aquarium supply store immediately. Commercial remedies are available but must be administered quickly. A salt bath with warm temperatures may be a temporary solution, because it may retard growth of the fungus. However, a salt bath won't cure the fish. More effective treatments are needed.

China Disease (highly contagious)

This is not a very common disease, and you must be absolutely certain of your diagnosis. This is the most contagious disease listed here, and the most deadly. There is no known cure for China disease.

The symptoms are very easy to diagnose. The tail fin and other fins begin to fray, very much as in fin rot. However, China disease begins at the

> **CAUTION**
>
> Oranda and Lionhead owners beware. In the spring or summer, a whitish film covers the heads of these fish. Be very discerning. More times than not, this is indicative of continued hood growth, not illness.

base of the tail fin and works its way outward. Also, the infected areas begin to blacken and even the ventral region turns black. Unfortunately, the infected fish must be painlessly destroyed and the other fish put in the hospital tank. A ten-day progressive salt treatment for the remaining fish is a good idea. In the meantime, you need to perform an emergency cleaning of the tank. This must be done immediately to prevent further damage by this disease.

Fin Congestion (contagious)

This disease very commonly attacks goldfish, especially the long-finned varieties. It is easily identifiable because of the red blotches that appear on the trailing edges of the fins. Look for hemorrhaging—bright-red areas on the surface of the fins. Be careful, though: Many goldfish have red blood vessels visible in their tails and this is normal. Goldfish infected with this disease have blood vessels that become inflamed at the ends of the tail. This disease starts at the edge of the fins and works its way toward the body, much like fin rot.

Fin congestion is an indication that the water quality in the tank is very poor. Change 50 percent of the water and add one tablespoon of salt for every gallon of water (sprinkle the salt around the tank over a period of a few minutes—don't just dump it all in). This treatment should clear up the problem in a few days. If this treatment doesn't work, you need to purchase an antibiotic, either penicillin or tetracycline hydrochloride. Follow the directions carefully, as these chemicals can become very toxic to the fish.

Fin or Tail Rot (contagious)

This is sometimes caused by fighting among your fish—the fins are damaged and bacteria then infect the injured area. Other times, the fish just contract it. It can also be triggered by poor water quality. It is easily detectable, as the fins have missing parts and eventually become shredded. As the disease worsens, the entire fin will be eaten away.

There are many broad-spectrum medications that will help you deal with this situation. Consult your local aquarium supply store dealer. Be sure to treat the aquarium water as well, because fin rot is usually contagious. Also, take the necessary steps to remedy the cause of the infection. Separate fish that cause injury to the fins and make sure water quality is at its best.

Fish Pox (probably not contagious)

This disease affects Koi more often than goldfish, but it's best to cover it in this chapter anyway. This is a viral infection that causes a milky white or pinkish

Your goldfish's fins should always be full and flowing. Any cramping or shredding is a sign of a problem.

gray waxy film to develop over the fish's skin and fins. The infection usually appears, gets worse, and then disappears.

It is not definitively known what triggers fish pox, or why it eventually disappears, but it does not appear to be contagious. Nonetheless, take the necessary precautions and isolate the infected fish until the film goes away. This will generally take seven to ten days. This ailment is more annoying than dangerous, since it does not kill the fish. However, there is no known cure.

Fungus (highly contagious)

The most common species of fungus infecting goldfish is *Saprolegnia*. It is a fuzzy growth that differs from velvet (see page 115) because it is whiter and easier to notice. The primary cause of this infection is damage to the mucous layer of the skin. This allows fungal spores to germinate and grow into the skin. Injury, environmental conditions, and parasites can damage the protective mucous layer.

Some experts paint the affected areas with methylene blue and place the fish in a ten-day salt-water treatment. Again, commercial treatments are usually available. The entire aquarium should be treated with a fungicide.

Furunculosis (contagious)

This bacterial infection can go unnoticed for some time, but then it spreads rapidly. These bacteria infect the flesh under the scales, somewhat like skin flukes (see page 114). The infection is first manifested by the appearance of bumps under the scales. A short time later, the bumps rupture and create large bleeding ulcers. That is why this ailment is sometimes referred to as ulcer disease. There is no certain cure.

Some experts argue that all foods should be changed immediately. If you have a trustworthy heater, you may want to raise the water to 80°F, as furunculosis is a cold-water disease and the high temperature is thought to kill it. While some fish have actually survived, large scars resulting from the infection often prove to be a problem. Fish with these kinds of ulcers should probably be destroyed.

Mouth Fungus (contagious)

This malady, also called Chondrococcus disease, is caused by the bacteria *Flexibacter* and manifests itself as a white, cottony growth on the mouth. It can infect the gills, back, and fins. If left untreated, this infection will destroy the entire mouth region of a goldfish and lead to death.

Some diseases are highly contagious. Isolate sick fish so they do not infect your whole tank.

Commercial cures are available, and I strongly suggest that you follow the directions to the letter. You can begin a salt-water bath right away if you are unable to find a treatment. Some people start a salt bath and then use a general commercial fungal or bacterial control. Consult your aquarium supply store owner once you have made your diagnosis.

Ulcers (highly contagious)

This infection tends to begin internally, then manifests itself as large red ulcers, boils, and dark reddening at the bases of the fins. It cannot be mistaken for anchor worm because anchor-worm ulcers swell up, whereas these tend to eat away into the body. That is why this ailment is sometimes referred to as hole-in-the-body disease.

A salt bath may be too harsh, but the infected fish should be isolated immediately and fed medicated food. Sometimes antibiotics and a veterinarian may be required. Consult your local aquarium supply store before proceeding.

Parasite Infestations

Anchor Worm (highly contagious)

These elongated crustaceans of the genus *Lernaea* attach to the skin of the fish. Several species of this parasite have been described, but all females have a head with an anchor shape that embeds in the flesh of the host. Instead of living on top of the scales, the anchor worm actually burrows into them. The fish will rub against anything in an attempt to scrape off the parasite. Like fish lice, these creatures cause irritation and localized bleeding at the point of attachment; from this protrudes a white worm that can sometimes grow quite long. Secondary bacterial infection can occur at these points.

Treating anchor worm includes taking the fish out of the water and removing the worm with forceps or tweezers. To remove the worm, place a wet cloth in your hand. Take hold of the fish in the hand holding the cloth. Make sure to position the fish so that the worm is facing you. With a pair of household tweezers, press as close to the ulcer as possible, but only extract the worm. Make sure not to rip any flesh off the fish and be careful not to break the parasite. This is very dangerous to the fish, and you must be extremely cautious when attempting this procedure. It may be best to get someone experienced to do it for you.

As in the case with fish lice, be sure to treat the infected area with an antiseptic after removing the parasite. In addition, antibiotic treatment may accelerate the healing of lesions. Consult your aquarium dealer for a general full-spectrum antibiotic.

Fish Lice (highly contagious)

There is no mistaking this ugly problem. These small, crab-like parasites measure about a fifth of an inch across. They are round, disk-shaped creatures that clamp onto a host and refuse to let go. The parasites can sometimes be found on fins, but these areas are usually not quite so satisfying as soft tissues such as the body and gills. Sometimes the infected fish will rub up against objects in the tank in an effort to scrape these pests off. Some fish have been known to jump out of the water trying to cleanse themselves of these ghastly crustaceans. After the parasite disengages, the part of the fish that has been bitten may become infected.

Fortunately, there are a number of quality commercial parasite-control products on the market. To treat fish lice, anchor worms, and leeches, Dipterex, Masoten, Dylox, or Nequvon are frequently recommended. Your aquarium supply store owner can help you select one. The fish should be quarantined and the tank disinfected with the same parasite-control product. Lice are extremely treatable, but both the fish and the aquarium must be treated.

On larger fish, experts have been known to drip hot paraffin wax from a candle onto the parasite. Usually this is enough to get the parasite to release its grasp. Other experts recommend giving the afflicted fish a bath for fifteen minutes in a mixture of potassium permanganate and water, which should be diluted until it is extremely light pink. Consult your local aquarium supply store owner first.

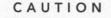

CAUTION

Do not use Formalin. Its margin for error is so slim that you will not only kill the parasites, you will more than likely kill your goldfish. This should be used by professionals only.

All bite marks or wounds on the fish must be treated. Dab a little Mercurochrome, malachite green, or methylene blue on the spot.

Ich (highly contagious)

Raised white spots about the size of salt granules that appear on the body and fins are the parasite *Ichthyophthirius*. This is one of the most common parasites among aquarium fish. It should not be taken lightly, as it will kill your fish if left untreated.

This ailment is so common that there are many commercial ich (pronounced *ick*) remedies on the market. Remove the fish showing the symptoms and treat it in a hospital tank. However, the entire main tank must also be treated. Follow the remedy directions carefully.

Parasites can attack your fish at any time. Look closely at the fish when you feed them to detect problems early on.

If a commercial ich treatment is not available to you, raise the hospital tank temperature to 85°F and add one teaspoon of salt for every gallon of water. Give the fish in the hospital tank the ten-day salt-water treatment. It is important to kill this organism before it has a chance to infest your entire population.

Leeches (highly contagious)

Leeches are another group of parasites that may be found on the skin and scales of your fish. They are relatively uncommon among goldfish but are serious once contracted. These are not the leeches we see as free-living creatures in lakes and ponds. Rather, these are parasitic, wormlike creatures that attach to your fish, feeding on flesh and blood. They need to be removed as quickly as possible but not with forceps or tweezers. These parasites are very strong, and you are likely

TIP

If the ich spots are only on the gills of your goldfish, your male goldfish may be coming into breeding season. In this case, watch your fish carefully to see if the white spots spread to the body. If not, your goldfish are not diseased, just a bit amorous.

Your aquarium supply dealer can help you choose effective remedies for many illnesses.

to do more damage to your fish than to the leeches by trying to pull them off. Call your aquarium supply store for advice about commercially produced cures.

Here is another solution: Prepare a salt bath consisting of eight level table-spoons of table salt for each gallon of water. Once the salt is sufficiently dissolved, add the fish for no more than ten minutes. The leeches that do not fall off can now be removed quite easily with tweezers or forceps.

Again, the aquarium needs to be treated immediately with commercial parasite-control chemicals. Check all your fish for parasites when one is discovered, and always isolate the infected fish.

Skin and Gill Flukes (highly contagious)

These flukes are microscopic parasites that lodge themselves in the gills. As with all infestations, weakened fish fall victim first. The gill fluke *(Dactylogyrus)* is easily detected. It causes the gills to swell up pink and red, and the fish spends a lot of time near the surface trying to get oxygen. Sometimes, a puslike fluid will be exuded from the gills at this time. Other symptoms include severe color loss, scratching, and labored respiration. The skin fluke *(Gyrodactylus)* gives the skin a swollen appearance. As in all other parasitic infestations, the host fish is constantly rubbing against objects to be rid of the pest.

Aquarium supply stores have pest-control remedies for this ailment, which is easier to treat than the others in this section. The tank also needs to be treated to make sure the infestation does not spread.

Velvet (highly contagious)

The parasite *Oodinium* causes a golden velvety coat on the body and fins that is referred to as velvet. This disease is very difficult to detect initially because the fuzzy area has a yellow or golden color, which is difficult to see on a goldfish. Commercial treatments for this fungus are best. Some experts use malachite green or the old-fashioned salt bath. If your aquarium supply store doesn't have a commercial treatment (which it should), I suggest the ten-day salt-water treatment. Also, make sure to place an antifungal chemical in the main aquarium to disinfect it.

Signs and Symptoms of Goldfish Diseases

Disease	Signs and Symptoms
Anchor worm	A white worm protrudes from a red, agitated area on the fish's body. Infested fish rubs against anything it can, attempting to scratch off the parasite.
Body slime fungus	Protective skin mucus grows white and starts peeling off, as if the fish were shedding or molting. Fins are eventually covered as well.
China disease	Tail fins and other fins begin to fray, beginning at the base of the fin and working outward. Infected areas begin to blacken. Ventral region begins to turn black.
Constipation, indigestion	Fish is very inactive, usually rests on the bottom of the tank. Abdominal swelling and bulging is likely.
Dropsy (kidney bloat)	Abdomen bloats noticeably. Scales stick out like pinecones.
Fin congestion	Blood vessels become inflamed at the ends of the tail fins. Starts at the edge of the fins and works toward the body.
Fin or tail rot	Fins have missing parts and eventually become shredded. Rays become inflamed and entire fin may be eaten away.
Fish lice	Round, disk-shaped, transparent crustaceans clamp onto fish and refuse to let go. Infected fish will rub against objects in the tank in an effort to remove the parasites.
Fish pox	Whitish or pinkish waxy film develops over fish's skin and fins.

Disease	Signs and Symptoms
Fungus	Fuzzy growth develops that is different from velvet because it is more whitish.
Furunculosis	Raised bumps form under the scales that eventually rupture and cause bleeding ulcers.
Gill fluke	Gills swell pink and red. Fish spends time at the surface gasping for air. Puslike fluid will be exuded from the gills.
Ich	Raised white spots about the size of salt granules appear on the body and fins.
Leeches	Long, wormlike parasites attach both ends to the fish and do not come off easily.
Mouth fungus	White cottony growth on mouth, sometimes spreading to the gills and other parts.
Pop-eye	Fish's eyes protrude from inflamed eye sockets.
Skin fluke	Localized swelling, excessive mucus, and ulcerations appear on the skin. The fish constantly tries to rid itself of these parasites by rubbing against aquarium objects.
Swim bladder disease	Fish swims on its sides, upside down, or somersaults through the water. Fish may be found either on the top or at the bottom of the tank.
Tumors	Obvious bumps, lumps, and protrusions appear that sometimes look like large blisters or warts.
Ulcers	Large red lesions, boils, dark reddening, and bleeding occur.
Velvet	Fuzzy yellow or golden areas appear.

Learning More About Your Goldfish

Goldfish enthusiasts and breeders number in the millions throughout the world. As you become more involved in goldfish keeping, you may be surprised at how many people share this avocation. The resources for the home aquarist are almost limitless, ranging from books to the Internet.

Books

Andrews, C., *Guide to Fancy Goldfishes*, Interpet Publishing, 2002.

DeVito, C., Skomal, G., *The Everything Tropical Fish Book*, Adams Media Corp., 2000.

Geran, J., *The Proper Care of Goldfish*, TFH Publications, 2000.

Goldfish Society of America, *The Official Guide to Goldfish*, TFH Publications, 1991.

Halls, Steve, *Your Healthy Garden Pond*, Howell Book House, 2000.

Johnson, E., Hess, R., *Fancy Goldfish: A Complete Guide to Care and Collecting*, New Holland Publishers, 2001.

Okamoto, K., Takaoka, K., Kuru, S., *Kingyo: The Artistry of Japanese Goldfish*, Kodansha International, 2004.

Skomal, G., *Koi: An Owner's Guide to a Happy Healthy Fish*, Howell Book House, 1999.

Smartt, J., Bundell, J., *Goldfish Breeding and Genetics*, TFH Publications, 1996.

Magazines

While there are not a lot of magazines committed solely to goldfish, popular fishkeeping magazines do run articles on goldfish from time to time. These articles provide you with some of the most up-to-date information on aquarium keeping. Timely articles on breeding, feeding, disease, and husbandry will both entertain and inform the new aquarist. Product information and classified advertising are excellent features of aquarium magazines.

Koi USA Magazine
P.O. Box 469070
Escondido, CA 92046-2073
(888) 660-2073
www.koiusa.com

Tropical Fish Hobbyist
TFH Publications Inc.
One TFH Plaza
Neptune City, NJ 07753
(800) 631-2188
www.tfhmagazine.com

Internet

The Internet is by far the fastest way to get and exchange information on goldfish. If you have access to the Internet, then you have unlimited access to a vast amount of information on these fish. You can get immediate advice about any aspect of keeping goldfish.

Aquarium Fish
www.aquariumfish.com
You'll find article archives from *Aquarium Fish International* magazine, polls, forums, products and photos.

Glimmering Goldfish
www.goldfishinfo.com
Great, in-depth information on care and keeping, varieties, history, water chemistry, and everything else to do with goldfish.

Goldfish Paradise
www.goldfishparadise.com
The Goldfish Paradise Society is a global community of goldfish enthusiasts at all levels. You'll find forums and Q&A areas, articles on all aspects of care, a gallery of photos, and much more.

The Goldfish Society of America
www.goldfishsociety.org
This site has information on GSA activities and goldfish events worldwide, plus links to local clubs.

Olympic Koi, Goldfish & Water Garden Club
www.olympickoiclub.org
This club promotes Koi keeping. The site includes great information about pond design and Koi care.

Practical Fishkeeping
www.practicalfishkeeping.co.uk
This is the web site of *Practical Fishkeeping*, a British magazine. There are article archives, product reviews, videos, blogs, a forum, and more.

Swimming Goldfish
swimming-goldfish.com
This is a clearinghouse of links to dealers who sell fish and supplies.

The Goldfish Net
p092.ezboard.com/The-Goldfish-Net/bthegoldfishnet
This is a discussion board about everything to do with goldfish. Discussions are sported by topics, making it very easy to find information.

Index

Photo Credits:

Tammy Rao: 1, 17, 19, 21, 27, 28, 30, 32, 34, 35, 37, 39, 40, 42, 44–45, 50, 52, 57, 60, 67, 73, 82, 86-87, 89, 90, 92, 94, 100, 105, 107, 108, 111, 112, 115, 116

Jean M. Fogle: 4–5, 8–9, 11, 13, 31, 63, 76, 77, 78, 88, 103

Teresa Lenihan: 14, 15, 22, 23, 24, 25, 46, 53, 55, 59, 65, 71, 72, 74, 75, 85, 97, 98

Howell Book House: 10, 48, 61, 69, 80, 83, 101